A Sense

of the

Supernatural

THE TEACHINGS OF KABBALAH SERIES

by Rabbi Yitzchak Ginsburgh

The Hebrew Letters
Channels of Creative Consciousness

The Mystery of Marriage
How to Find True Love and Happiness in Married Life

Awakening the Spark Within
Five Dynamics of Leadership that can Change the World

Transforming Darkness into Light
Kabbalah and Psychology

Rectifying the State of Israel
A Political Platform based on Kabbalah

Living in Divine Space
Kabbalah and Meditation

Body, Mind, and Soul
Kabbalah on Human Physiology, Disease, and Healing

Consciousness & Choice
Finding Your Soulmate

The Art of Education
Internalizing Ever-New Horizons

What You Need to Know About Kabbalah

Kabbalah and Meditation for the Nations

Anatomy of the Soul

A Sense of the Supernatural
Interpretation of Dreams and Paranormal Experiences

A SENSE

OF THE

SUPERNATURAL

INTERPRETATION OF DREAMS
AND PARANORMAL EXPERIENCES

A SELECTION OF PERSONAL RESPONSA

FROM

RABBI YITZCHAK GINSBURGH

ג	ל	ע	י	נ	י
ה	ט	י	ב	א	ו
נ	פ	ל	א	ו	ת
מ	ת	ו	ר	ת	ד

Gal Einai
Jerusalem • New York • Los Angeles

A Sense of the Supernatural

Rabbi Yitzchak Ginsburgh

Printed in the United States of America and Israel
First Edition

Israel: GAL EINAI
         PO Box 1015
         Kfar Chabad 72915
         tel. (in Israel): 1-700-700-966
         tel. (from abroad): 972-3-9608008
email: books@inner.org
Web: www.inner.org

GAL EINAI produces and publishes books, pamphlets,
audiocassettes and videocassettes by Rabbi Yitzchak
Ginsburgh. To receive a catalog of our products in English
and/or Hebrew, please contact us at any of the above
addresses, email orders@inner.org or call our orders
department in Israel.

ISBN: 978-965-7146-25-5

text layout: David Hillel

cover design: Shmuel Kaffe

TABLE OF CONTENTS

PREFACE

THROUGHOUT OUR LIVES, phenomena that baffle and perplex us magnify themselves in our consciousness and then fade, leaving us to question their true meaning: strange coincidences, dreams with seemingly significant meanings, or even a sense of tapping into other worlds, to name but a few. We may try to push these experiences out of our minds or remain confounded by their elusive significance, but either way, we remain with the uneasy feeling that there is more to the experience than we can fathom.

Chassidut teaches us how to accept these phenomena with equanimity and simple faith, while offering us a clear directive in interpreting and integrating them into our essentially physical day-to-day lives, without becoming overwhelmed by their apparent "weirdness."

In general, by relating the symbols in our spiritual experiences to authentic Torah ideas, we can discover how to integrate these insights in our efforts to form a positive relationship with our Creator. By correctly meditating upon the meaning of such incidents, we can enhance our understanding of how to correct and clarify our inner character traits.

It is our hope that studying the replies in this volume will provide you with a new, fuller and clearer attitude towards perceiving and interpreting the spiritual phenomena that you may experience and with the knowledge necessary for integrating the lessons that God is continuously transmitting through His creation. Nonetheless, it should be made clear that true understanding of the supernatural can only be achieved through constant striving for personal improvement together with intense study of Torah and Chassidut.

With the coming of Mashiach, we will enter an era of redemption that will be distinguished by a new spiritual awareness that will permeate human consciousness, in which life will be experienced as a constantly miraculous revelation of Divine Providence. Learning how to decipher supernatural phenomena such as those explored in this book, and how to incorporate them into our every day lives, can therefore serve as a catalyst to achieving the ultimate fulfillment of our mission on earth and to witnessing the ushering in of a new era to all of mankind.

Since its launching in the year 5756 (1996), Gal Einai's website has been visited by hundreds of thousands of surfers on the web. Since 5757, when an email address was opened for questions to Rabbi Ginsburgh, thousands of letters have poured into Rabbi Ginsburgh's mailbox from all over the world. The questions received by Rabbi Ginsburgh were many and varied, asking for enlightenment and advice on any of a multitude of subjects ranging from personal advice to questions concerning society in general; questions by Jews knowledgeable in Torah and those with little or no Jewish education at all as well as by non-Jews who affiliate themselves with Judaism and those who have previously had little or no contact with the Jewish faith.

This volume is the first of a series of volumes of personal responsa dealing with questions concerning spiritual and psychic incidents, dream interpretation and other symbolic phenomena. Other volumes of questions and answers, presently in the planning, cover a variety of topics such as: meditation and spiritual healing; health and medicine; Torah, Kabbalah and Chassidut; Kabbalah and mathematics; relationships and personal advice; righteous gentiles and righteous converts; current events, Israel and the redemption.

The original letters have been edited for brevity, clarity, and in order to conceal the identity of the author. Some letters containing similar questions have been consolidated. Rabbi Ginsburgh has greatly expanded his original replies and extended endnotes have been added, spicing the letters with Chassidic stories, explanations of certain concepts as well as elaboration on the themes mentioned in the letters, together with relevant sources. In this way, the endnotes supply a wealth of additional material suited for both the layman and the more seasoned student of Chassidut.

In this volume we have followed the same conventions as those used in past publications. A particularly useful survey of these conventions can be found in *The Mystery of Marriage*. Nonetheless, it is particularly important to note that when "GOD" (in small-caps) is used it is in specific reference to His essential Name, *Havayah* (i.e., the Tetragrammaton). Otherwise, "God" can refer to any of the sanctified Names of the Almighty, a discussion of which, along with many other newer conventions, can be found in *What You Need to Know About Kabbalah.*

A comprehensive glossary has been included at the back of the book to aid the reader in understanding unfamiliar terms that may appear in the book. Indexes have also been added to assist the reader in his quest for knowledge on a particular subject.

Special thanks to Mr. David Shirel, who founded and ran the Gal-Einai website for nearly a decade; Mrs. Shelli Karzan, who edited replies to Rabbi Ginsburgh's mail during the time that the mailbox was running; Mrs. Uriela Sagiv and Mrs. Sara Esther Crispe for their original editing of the letters into book form and for their proofreading of the final text. Thanks also to Rabbi Moshe Genuth for his important editorial input; and to Mrs. Rachel Gordon, for editing the present, expanded version of the book.

Letter 1

Mystical Experiences

For some years now, I have been aware that I have the ability to tap into other worlds and experience various paranormal events. However, sometimes these experiences scare me, and I wonder if I am not tapping into magic or sorcery and whether I should try to work to eliminate these experiences from my life, and if so, how?

Just as a person is composed of a physical body that is imbued with a spiritual soul, so too, the physical world in which we live is imbued with spiritual levels not usually apparent to us. At times when we tap into these higher spiritual levels the experience may be scary, similar to the experience of setting out to sea or of advancing into unknown territory. Nevertheless, with the guidance offered us by the Torah, our God-given "map," we have nothing to fear, neither in our every-day lives nor in the extraordinary occurrences that we may sometimes encounter. Indeed, the Ba'al Shem Tov taught us to fear nothing besides God Himself.

The verse in the Torah which best provides an authentic Jewish approach towards the types of experience that you describe is, "Be wholehearted with GOD your God."[3] This precept concludes a series of verses that deal with the prohibitions against witchcraft, sorcery and other pagan practices.[4] Since these practices were widespread among the people who resided in Canaan when the nation of Israel claimed the land, they presented one of the principal obstacles to promoting Torah values and practices in the hearts of the people. The Divine antidote to these insidious influences is identified in the verse as the attribute of wholeheartedness or sincerity (תמימות).[5]

The Torah's abhorrence of occult practice does not imply that a person with unusual sensitivities to spiritual experiences, like you, need ignore, suppress or devalue them. They certainly possess a place, even a

We find stories of many righteous people, who possessed psychic powers, yet at some stage in their lives they asked God to remove these phenomena from them. One such example is the Komarna Rebbe, who in his youth would see each sage who he mentioned in his Talmudic study appear before him. He would describe each one to his study partner in detail. The Komarna Rebbe beseeched God to remove this power from him for it disturbed him from wholehearted devotion to God in study and prayer.[1]

Another example is the Seer of Lublin who told his followers that at first he was able to see from one end of the world to the other. However, not being able to stand seeing so much evil in the world, he requested that this power be taken from him. Even so, he still retained the spiritual power to see eight-hundred-thousand(!) times further than the average person.[2]

prominent one, when dealt with appropriately and incorporated within a Torah-oriented way of life.[6] However, if the experiences disturb your simple, devoted service of God, then you should try to suppress their effects and beseech God to remove these super-rational phenomena from you.[7]

One of the most basic teachings of the Ba'al Shem Tov, the eighteenth century founder of the Chassidic movement, asserts that, as we move through life, we are constantly being addressed by God through both our normal and paranormal senses.[8] Although it may not appear this way to most people, it is only because a person does not activate the spiritual side of his consciousness that it remains hidden from awareness. Indeed, at every moment we can make a conscious choice to identify with the more concealed aspects of our existence and thereby penetrate the inner dimension of physical reality.[9]

It is indicated in various Jewish teachings that all of God's creations are endowed with such a spiritual consciousness. In particular, in the mystical collection of verses called *Perek Shirah* ("The Chapter of Song"), we find that every creature is gifted with a unique song of praise to its Creator, which describes the essence of its spiritual consciousness.[10]

So, in fact, every experience in life has some providential significance of which, unfortunately, we cannot always be certain without the benefit of direct prophecy. Although this appears to leave us in a paradoxical situation, experiencing a constant influx of Divine communication that we are not always able to decipher, Kabbalah teaches us that we can always benefit from these signals by adopting a dual strategy: the innocent path of wholeheartedness together with the focused approach of rational analysis.[11]

These two somewhat antithetical approaches to paranormal experiences work together as follows:

Whenever subliminal vibrations emanating from the spiritual realm amplify themselves in our consciousness, we must make a concentrated effort to accept them with equanimity, without becoming obsessed or overly concerned about the experience. In true simplicity, we should remember that all experiences ultimately emanate from God and thus are equally "normal." The danger lies in entertaining the possibility that such an experience emanates from some source other than God.

Having accepted the experience with true simplicity, we can then try to analyze the symbols that appear in the experience with the rational tools that are available to us and to attempt to relate the experience to legitimate Torah principles.

The very association in your mind with magic and sorcery is liable to totally pollute that which may otherwise be a potentially enriching spiritual experience, for the essence of the occult is denial of God's absolute unity and His mastery over creation.[12] Thus, practically speaking, the permissibility of opening yourself up to the sensations you describe depends upon the degree to which you can rid yourself of such associations.

To a certain extent, the simple indulgence of the ego in such an experience can be just as threatening as the introduction of occult associations. You should never consciously intend to bring on such an experience for the sake of the gratification it provides you, nor for the feeling of power it gives you. Doing so is a guarantee for either losing your sensitivity altogether, or for summoning all kinds of false experiences which are liable to have a destructive impact upon yourself and upon others.[13]

So don't attempt to intentionally seek out paranormal stimulation. When it presents itself, take it lightly, and try not to exaggerate its significance. In short, be wholehearted in your approach to life and you will find joy in having creation sing to you even when the words of the song are unclear. The essence of the song is the melody, and the melody is that our loving Father is with us at all times.

At the same time, realize that man's Divine gift of rational analysis is intended to help human beings digest experience so that the moral good that is inherent in it can be gleaned and the evil discarded. The process of rational analysis, clarifying reality through the prism of our consciousness,[14] occupies a central place in the Kabbalistic scheme of redemption. The Torah is our representation of the Divine standards intended to be applied in the pursuit of such clarity. Through the process of clarification we gradually strip away the layers of illusion that envelop reality and lay bare the Divine essence inherent in all things.

Hence it is incumbent upon you to try to refine and clarify your intuitive experience as best you can, using the language and thought patterns of the Torah as a guide.

The teachings of the Torah encompass law (*mitzvot* and *halachah*) as well as prayer, ethics, Kabbalah, Chassidut and much more.[15] The spiritual phenomena that you mention lend themselves in particular to the language and teachings of Kabbalah. Chassidic teachings, which enclothe Kabbalah in an accessible, conceptual form, can surely help you place your experiences into a proper perspective. Even familiarizing yourself with stories about the great Chassidic masters (especially the Ba'al Shem Tov) will demonstrate to you how relevant and prevalent experiences such as those you describe were to Jews who lived less than three hundred years ago.[16]

The stories and parables told by the great Chassidic Master, Rebbe Nachman of Breslov,[17] are another rich resource for you to explore in pursuing an alternative spiritual language with which to analyze your experience.[18]

With blessings of the Torah and the Land of Israel,

Notes:

1. See *Admorei Komarna, Megillat Setarim* p. 29b.

2. *Emunat Tzadikim* p. 63.

3. Deuteronomy 18:13.

4. The complete passage reads, "For you are coming into the land which GOD your God is giving you, do not learn to do as the abominations of those nations. There shall not be found amongst you one who passes his son and his daughter through fire [a form of idol

worship], nor one who practices divination, nor interprets temporal omens, nor a speculator, nor a sorcerer. Nor a snake-charmer, nor a medium, nor an oracle, nor one who consults the dead. Be wholehearted with GOD your God" (Ibid. 18:11-13).

Each of these forbidden practices is interpreted by Rashi (in his commentary on these verses) and Maimonides (*Mishneh Torah, Hilchot Avodah Zarah* 11:4-16). We will summarize these two interpretations in the chart below:

Term used in verse	Rashi	Maimonides
diviner (קֹסֵם קְסָמִים)	someone who uses a stick to receive "yes" or "no" replies to simple questions, such as whether to set out on a journey or not	someone who does any (repetitive) action to reach a state of blank-mindedness until he tells the future or offers advice
interpreter of temporal omens (מְעוֹנֵן)	someone who claims to know which time is propitious to begin a project etc., or simply a trickster by sleight of hand	an astrologer who says that a particular day is good or bad, such-and-such a time is good or bad for a particular task; similarly, someone who practices deception and allegedly acts as if he did something when he did not actually do it
speculator (מְנַחֵשׁ)	someone who claims to understand the propitious significance of superstitious signs, such as when bread falls from his mouth, a deer crosses his path, or his stick falls from his hand	as Rashi; also, one who interprets the chirping of the birds or the crowing of a cockerel or hen, or one who sets up signs for himself, saying, "if such-and-such happens, I will do so-and-so"
sorcerer (מְכַשֵּׁף)	[no explanation]	someone who performs spells

snake charmer (חֹבֵר חָבֶר)	someone who collects serpents or scorpions or other animals to one place	someone who uses insignificant "magic" words, gestures or items to arrest the injurious power of snakes etc.
medium (שֹׁאֵל אוֹב)	someone who conjures up the dead in his underarm	[no explanation]
oracle (יִדְּעֹנִי)	someone who puts the bone of a particular animal into his mouth and the bone "speaks"	[no explanation]
one who consults the dead (וְדֹרֵשׁ אֶל הַמֵּתִים)	someone who summons up the dead (to ask them questions), either onto his male organ or by using a human skull	someone who starves himself and sleeps in the graveyard or one who uses various other procedures, in order that a dead person will appear to him in a dream to answer his questions

These eight forbidden occult practices correspond to the eight impure creeping creatures mentioned in the Torah (Leviticus 11:29-30) as follows:

impure creeping creature	forbidden occult practice
weasel	diviner
mouse	interpreter of temporal omens
toad	speculator
hedgehog	sorcerer
mastigure	snake charmer
lizard	medium
chameleon	oracle
mole	one who consults the dead

5. Three interpretations of the attribute of *temimut* (תְּמִימוּת), which we have translated in general as, "wholeheartedness" in the context of the above-mentioned verse are those of Maimonides, Nachmanides and Rashi:

Maimonides considers *temimut* to be total disbelief in the spiritual powers attributed to the various types of witchcraft etc. (*Mishneh Torah, Hilchot Avodah Zarah* 11:16).

Nachmanides explains that *temimut* is to believe that even though God has empowered certain laws to govern the world, He Himself is above all of the laws that He has set, and He can change the course of nature as He wills.

Rashi's explanation is, "Walk with Him wholeheartedly, and wait for Him. Do not investigate future forecasts, rather, all that happens to you accept wholeheartedly, and then you will be with Him, and will be His portion." See below, Letter 15, note 1; see also at length the first part of our book (in Hebrew) *Tom Vada'at*.

6. The passage quoted at the beginning of note 2, above, continues with the verse, "A prophet from your brethren amongst you, as I [Moses] am, shall GOD your God establish for you; him shall you heed" (Deuteronomy 18:15). The ultimate spiritual experience is that of true prophecy!

    In Biblical times, those who desired to become prophets would join a school of prophecy where they would learn the correct way to become channels to the Divine will (see *Mishneh Torah, Hilchot Yesodei Hatorah*, Ch. 7). Even so, not all those who studied and practiced these teachings would be privileged to become true prophets of God. In modern times, the way to achieving genuine spirituality is by studying the Torah at all its levels and by observing its commandments. Jewish history is replete with individuals who have achieved great spiritual heights by serving God in this way. Studying Chassidut and living by its teachings, as exemplified by the great Chassidic masters, is particularly conducive to reaching heightened levels of spiritual awareness.

7. See Letter 3.

8. See Rabbi Shmuel Schneersohn (*Admor Moharash*), *Torat Shmuel* 5640, vol. II, p. 803, based on the Talmudic statement, "Even though he did

not see it [physically], his soul-root saw it [at a spiritual level]" (*Megilah* 3a).

9. The choice of whether or not to identify with the spiritual aspect of reality is actually the choice between life or death, good or evil (see Deuteronomy 30:19). The spiritual aspect of creation is the Divine life-force that vitalizes the material aspect of this world. Without the spiritual life-force the physical aspect of this world would be totally lifeless (Rabbi Shneur Zalman of Liadi, *Torah Or, Ki Tisah* 85c). The way to achieve this constant identification with the spiritual, while continuing to function normally even by material standards, is outlined in the teachings of the Ba'al Shem Tov and his followers. This is the service alluded to and encapsulated in the concluding phrase of the very first verse of the Torah, "[In the beginning God created] the heavens and the earth," alluding to the ability to be simultaneously present, in one's consciousness, in the heavens (i.e., the spiritual realm) and the earth (i.e., physical, mundane reality).

10. *Perek Shirah* is an ancient text, attributed to King David, composed of Biblical verses that articulate the songs of creation to God.

   There are four opinions as to who actually sings these verses of praise:

   a. All of God's creations—animals, plants and natural forces—literally sing to God.

   b. Above every physical creation there is a spiritual source, a celestial "prince," that governs it. It is this angelic minister who sings the song of the creation that it governs.

   c. The soul of man has a higher source than that of the angels. God imbued man, a complete miniature world, with an inherent awareness of all of His creations and instructed him to name them (Genesis 2:19). Man studies nature in order to learn about himself; he thus identifies with each of God's creations and serves as the mouthpiece of each to praise Him.

   d. God, the Creator, by knowing Himself, knows all of His creations and sings to Himself the song of each creation.

See our book (in Hebrew), *Adamah, Shamayim Ve'Tehom*, Introduction to *Perek Shirah*, pp. 220-255 for an in-depth discussion on these four levels.

11. This idea can be gleaned from the two names of Jacob. The name יעקב (Jacob), which can be divided into י and עקב (meaning "heel"), represents walking in the path of holistic simplicity; and ישראל (Israel), the letters of which permute to form the words לי ראש, "I possess a head," representing rational analysis. As a person humbly walks away from his spiritual experience in all simplicity, his mind is better able to analyze and appreciate from afar the true significance of his experience.

12. See *Nachmanides*, commentary on Deuteronomy 18:10-11.

13. Excessive egoism is the most destructive character trait. The Ba'al Shem Tov taught that God "dwells" within us even if we sink to the depths of impurity, yet of the egoist we are told, "I [God] and he cannot dwell together" (see *Sotah* 5a). Moreover, the Ba'al Shem Tov taught that the majority of deranged people became so as a result of their excessive and uncompromising pride; unable to achieve the full extent of their arrogant desires they became insane.

14. One of the principal teachings of the Ba'al Shem Tov is that every process of rectification must proceed through three stages: submission, separation and sweetening. The service of clarification belongs to the stage of separation. It was this stage that Adam, the first man, neglected in his service of God; it caused him to sin and resulted in punishment. See *The Mystery of Marriage*, p. 394, footnote 51.

15. In Kabbalah and Chassidut, studying the various levels of Torah is compared to walking through a pomegranate orchard. The word for orchard in Hebrew is פרדס, which is an acronym for the four general levels of Torah study (פשט, רמז, דרוש, סוד; literal meaning, allusions, homiletic expansion and secrets). The fact that the orchard is, in particular, a pomegranate orchard, alludes to the fact that all Jews (even the "sinners" amongst us) are as full of *mitzvot* as a

pomegranate is full of seeds, the edible part of the fruit (*Berachot* 57a). A ripe, fully developed pomegranate contains 613 seeds—613 being the exact number of commandments that the Jewish nation is commanded to observe!

The pomegranate is the fifth of the seven species with which the Land of Israel is blessed and thus corresponds to the *sefirah* of acknowledgment (הוד), the inner power of which is wholehearted sincerity or simplicity (תמימות), the subject of this letter. The word הוד also relates to וידוי, confession, which is the one practical requirement for true rectification of our actions and return to God's service. [The other two requirements are resolving never to commit the same sin again and regretting the sin (*Mishneh Torah, Hilchot Teshuvah*, 2:3).]

All levels of the Torah were given to **all** of us, however, the *ba'al teshuvah* (one who corrects his behavior through his desire to return to wholehearted commitment to Torah values and *mitzvot*) must attach himself in particular to the secrets of the Torah in order to achieve the level of motivation and inspiration that he needs to walk through the orchard and return to his Creator.

16. See our book in Hebrew, *Or Yisrael*, on the stories of the Ba'al Shem Tov with elucidations.

17. Rebbe Nachman of Breslov, *Sippurei Ma'asiot Mishanim Kadmoniot* ("Fables from Bygone Years").

18. In one of Rebbe Nachman's lesser known stories, he tells of a righteous Jew who raised himself to great spiritual heights by merely rejoicing in being Jewish. During this state of elation he experienced himself moving thousands and thousands of miles in the spiritual worlds, far away from where he had started. Nonetheless, when he landed, he was greatly surprised to discover that he was still in exactly the same place from which he had begun. Perhaps he had moved a hairsbreadth. Rebbe Nachman explains from this story that in God's eyes, the slightest movement that a person advances in this world, be it even less than a hairsbreadth, is even more valuable than

moving thousands of miles in the upper worlds (the story appears at the end of Rebbe Nachman's *Sippurei Ma'asiot,* see previous note).

In the context of our reply to this letter, we can learn three ideas from this story:

a. One of the primary prerequisites for experiencing genuine spirituality is joy (there are several examples of persona in the Bible who reached spiritual heights through experiencing joy brought on by listening to music). In Kabbalah, there is a direct relationship between joy, the inner power of the *sefirah* of understanding, and holistic simplicity, the inner power of the *sefirah* of acknowledgment. This finds expression in the phrase, "[the *sefirah* of] understanding extends to [the *sefirah* of] acknowledgment" [*Tikunei Zohar,* intro. (7a); *Etz Chayim,* 35:4].

b. Genuine spiritual experience depends upon the sweetening of the severe judgments associated with the left axis of the Tree of Life. When rectified, the left axis draws the soul upward to experience true spirituality. It begins with joy and concludes with holistic simplicity. When the joy of understanding extends to the *sefirah* of acknowledgment, it passes through the *sefirah* of might and sweetens all severe judgments,.

c. Although under the influence of a spiritual experience it may seem that things in the physical world are changing to the same extent as our spiritual meanderings, in reality this is not necessarily the case.

In our service of God, our movements in this world are of far greater importance than all that we can ever experience in the spiritual worlds. This idea is mentioned in the Mishnah in the name of Rabbi Jacob, "He would say, one hour of repentance and good deeds in this world is better than all of the pleasure of the World to Come" (*Avot* 4:22). Nachmanides, in the introduction to his commentary on the Book of Job, goes even further to say that seventy years of suffering as Job suffered are of no consequence compared to one hour of suffering of the soul in *Gehinom* (Hell). Thus even when we are suffering physically in this world, we can still reach great heights of joy (the joy that comes with understanding) by being thankful that we are being punished in this world and we will not have to suffer for our sins in the World to Come (*Tanya, Igeret Hateshuvah* ch. 12). Thanksgiving and acknowledgment that all is for the good are manifestations of the *sefirah* of acknowledgment (הוד), and they implement the state of natural consciousness that motivates our walking wholeheartedly in God's ways.

MANIPULATING NATURE

Someone driving with me for several hours noticed that we never once hit a red light. Since he knew that I can do bio-energetic manipulations in healing, he asked me if I was using my powers for this purpose. I wasn't aware that it was possible to do so. But if it is, am I allowed under Jewish law to do things such as stop the rain or change the light on purpose?

As I am planning to come soon to Israel, I am also wondering how my special gifts might be affected by the Holy Land.

FIRST, WE MUST REMEMBER that the laws of nature are an integral part of God's creation and are Divinely ordained and that, as a rule, God desires that the world follow its natural course.[1] Indeed, what actually happens in our world is largely dependent upon laws of probability, as known to modern science. He also desires that we pray to Him to change, for what we believe to be better, nature's probable course of events. Indeed, the only permissible manner to constructively affect the physical order is through prayer. (Clearly, the word "manipulate" in this context carries negative connotations and should best be avoided.)

Sometimes God wills to make the improbable happen, in order that we become aware of His Providence.

The Talmud[2] attributes the wondrous acts of healing wrought by the prophet Elisha, the greatest wonder-worker of the Bible,[3] as having been accomplished solely through the power of prayer.[4]

Balaam, a non-Jewish prophet hired by Balak, King of Moab, tried to curse the nation of Israel before they entered the Holy Land. However, each time he tried to curse them, God turned his curse into a blessing.[5] In contrast to Elisha, the Talmud[6] teaches us that Balaam used witchcraft in order to manipulate the laws of nature. Through his impure powers, Balaam reached similar heights of prophecy to those reached by Moses. Yet, Balaam abused his powers, while the Jewish prophets use their spiritual powers to bring their brethren closer to God.[7]

God created man with the freedom to choose between good and evil, and to influence nature either positively or negatively. Indeed, through his choice, man can either bring life or death to the world. For example, in the Talmud we are taught that someone born under the astrological influence of Mars will have an instinctive disposition to bloodshed. However, the Talmud also states that he has the power to choose whether to shed blood for evil purposes (slaying people, God-forbid), for neutral purposes (as a butcher), or for matters of holiness (as a *mohel*, who performs the commandment to circumcise Jewish males). Thus, by his freedom of choice, a person has the power to influence the natural course of humanity for better or, God-forbid, for worse. Even so, through heartfelt prayer a Jew even has the capability to change the effects of such an astrological influence.[8]

Since heartfelt prayer is within the power of each and every person, regardless of his or her spiritual level, anyone can theoretically become a channel for God's will to influence nature. In fact, many of the accounts in the Talmud of wonder-workers involve ordinary Jews who achieved their power through nothing more than prayer.[9]

Hence the conscious realization that a person possesses psychic potential, should not lead that person (or others) to think that he or she is innately different from anyone else with regard to the ability to inspire Divine intervention within the created realm.

In truth, the service of diligent commandment performance and Torah study can be just as effective as prayer in inspiring God's miraculous intervention within the natural order.[10] Therefore, although prayer affords us the opportunity to concentrate on influencing Divine will in a particular way, we may indeed be better off leaving such determinations up to God, increasing our Torah observance and good deeds instead.

We are told of many Chassidic masters who possessed supernatural psychic powers, yet prayed that these very powers be taken from them. This was because they realized that such powers could actually impede their wholehearted service of God and prevent them from realizing their true mission in life.[11]

The Divine mission entrusted to every Jew is to spread the Torah's light and wisdom throughout the world by means of the natural channels afforded him by his conscious mind and talents. One's deepest insights, too, can only be broadcast when conveyed through normal channels of communication. For example, someone with a talent for music can express himself through playing or composing music or song; someone with artistic talents can express his insights through the medium of art or poetry and the like. A person who attempts to tap into the energies of the paranormal realm in order to transmit insights or other forms of experience will at best succeed in influencing a very small circle of people, and at worst may end up losing his or her own spiritual direction.

It is to your merit that you seek guidance in relation to the psychic powers that you sense inside you. By so doing, it is clear that you recognize the primacy of Torah in shaping your path of Divine service.

Practically speaking, the first guideline you should adopt is to refrain from praying that God use you as an instrument for changing the natural order. The Talmud teaches that, as a rule, even God refrains from intervening in the natural realm.[12] This should, of course, discourage you from attempting to use your abilities to manipulate the weather or other natural phenomena.[13] Instead, you should make every effort to channel your spiritual powers into the service of heartfelt prayer to God for things that you know to be good.

Regarding your question concerning the influence of the Land of Israel in this regard, according to many sources, the atmosphere of the Land of Israel is considered to render one especially sensitive to Divine influence, as we are taught, "The air of the Land of Israel makes a person wiser."[14] In the Talmud we find that a person does not sin unless a spirit of folly enters him.[15] The air of the Land of Israel assists a person so that he should not be tempted into performing questionable acts by such a moment of foolishness.[16]

Entering the Land of Israel is entering Divine space; a space encompassing us from all sides that is favorable for perceiving Divine inspiration. The holy atmosphere of the Land of Israel is conducive to illuminating even the most concealed nuances of mistaken thinking, thereby allowing us to uproot them from our psyches.[17] These mistaken ways of thinking are the subtlest forms of spiritual idolatry that stem from either conscious or unconscious reliance on natural causation—the mindspace of the Diaspora.[18] In the land of Israel, we should make even more of a conscious effort to see how Divine Providence guides us, for the land of Israel is, "a land that GOD, your God, looks after; the eyes of GOD, your God, are always upon it, from the year's beginning until the year's end."[19]

The fourth Lubavitcher Rebbe, Rabbi Shmuel Schneersohn, once said that a simple Jew in the Land of Israel may be on a higher level of spiritual consciousness than a great Torah scholar outside the land, and that this higher level is reflected by his enhanced ability to change the course of nature for the better through heartfelt prayer.

We can glean additional insights that relate to the issue of psychic power from Chassidic teachings. For example, there is a Talmudic dictum that states that one's thoughts and intentions can have a tangible effect upon reality.[21] This concept is interpreted more extensively by the Chassidic masters. The previous Rebbe[22] cited

The following anecdote indicates how the previous Rebbe extricated his chassidim from Russia by his power of concentrated thought:

At the festive meal of the eighth day of Sukot, the Rebbe Rayatz spoke of the power of thought to act on reality. At some point in the proceedings, a young man who had been a follower of the Rebbe in Russia and had successfully reached Riga (where the Rebbe resided at that time) during that year, asked, "What do we gain from this?" (i.e. what benefit is there in the power of thought?). The Rebbe then replied, "Very great benefit." After a long moment of silence, the Rebbe asked the young man, "And where were you last year on Sukot?"[20]

this principle in support of the idea that one can overcome natural limitations through the power of thought,[23] especially in helping other souls release themselves from situations of oppression or captivity.

The power of thought can even be more profound than the power of vision, as we can understand from the common experience of sensing someone staring at us even when they are hidden from view.[24] Moreover, two souls, separated by both time and distance, can suddenly find themselves "face-to-face" when re-oriented through the spiritual power of thought.[25] This is why Chassidic Rebbes, besides the prayers that they pray in order to arouse Heavenly compassion for each of their disciples, also take time to think of each of their disciples and contemplate them with love. In this way, the Rebbe similarly arouses his disciples' love for him.[26] Merely by concentrating one's thoughts lovingly on another, one is in essence offering up a prayer that inspires God to react compassionately towards that person as well.

One of the most fundamental teachings of the Ba'al Shem Tov states that, "In the place where a man's will and thoughts are, that is where he is."[27] This means that one's thought must be directed through his will. In scientific terminology this can be understood to mean that the power of will transforms thought into a vector force that directs Divine energy into the physical world at the point where it is most needed.

With blessings of the Torah and the Land of Israel,

📜 Notes:

1. The Name of God, *Elokim* (א‑להים), is the Name used in the first chapter of Genesis, which describes the act of creation. The word א‑להים can be divided into the two words אל הים, which mean "to the sea." This alludes to the natural course which nature follows, just as all rivers flow towards the sea. See also, Letter 8, note 2.

2. *Megilah* 27a.

3. The numerical value of the name *Elisha* (אלישע) in Hebrew, is equal to the numerical value of the phrase meaning, "something from nothing" (יש מאין). This equivalence indicates Elisha's power to emulate God in the act of creation *ex nihilo* through the power of prayer, which arouses a new will in the Creator, as it were, to create reality anew (as in the case of totally healing a terminal disease). The meaning of *Elisha* in Hebrew is, in fact, "God of salvation."

4. In Aramaic, prayer is called *rachmei*, which literally means, "compassion." Our prayers have the power to arouse the compassion of *Rachmana*, the Merciful One.

5. Numbers, chs. 22-24.

6. *Sanhedrin* 105a.

7. *Bamidbar Rabah* 20:1.

8. *Shabbat* 156a. This level of understanding the concept of astrological influence (מזל) is the third and lowest interpretation of the phrase, "There is no astrological influence upon Israel." Above this interpretation is the understanding that the spiritual root of the souls of Israel emanates from a source that is above all astrological influences, meaning that the nation of Israel as a whole is not governed by the limits of nature.

   The highest level of interpreting this phrase is according to the rule of the Ba'al Shem Tov, who, by exchanging the vowels of the first word would render it, "[Divine] nothingness is the astrological influence of Israel," meaning that the light that shines directly from God is the spiritual source of the Jewish people. This level is particularly manifest during the Hebrew month of Adar, of which it is said, "Its astrological influence is prosperous" (*Ta'anit*, 29b).

9. Examples of such incidences can be found in *Ta'anit*, 25a-26b.

10. In particular, giving charity is known to have a life-saving quality that is capable of overriding the astrological influence that a person has (*Shabbat* 156b; see also note 8, above), as in the verse, "Charity saves from death." This phrase appears twice in the Book of

Proverbs. The first time in the verse, "The treasures of evil are of no avail, but charity saves from death" (Proverbs 10:2) and the second time in the verse, "Wealth will be of no avail on the day of wrath, but charity saves from death" (*ibid.* 11:4).

11. See Letter 3.

12. *Berachot* 58a.

13. Another story about the Komarna Rebbe (see framed inset in Letter 1), is that as a child, he once met a butcher in the marketplace who was about to buy an animal for slaughtering. The boy told the butcher that he should not buy the animal because it was a *treifah* (it would not survive the year and would therefore be found non-kosher once slaughtered). The butcher asked the boy to tell him which animal he should buy and gave him a coin for his services. The boy's choice proved correct, and the butcher continued to make use of the boy's insight and to pay him for his services. When the child's father heard of this, he told him not to use his powers for such things.

14. *Bava Batra* 158b.

15. *Sotah* 3a.

16. Rabbi Menachem Mendel Schneersohn, *Igrot Kodesh*, vol. 2, 255.

17. *Avodah Zarah* 45b.

18. See our book *Living in Divine Space*, ch. 10 and notes.

19. Deuteronomy 11:12.

20. *Ibid.* See also, *Torat Menachem*, v. 7, p. 359.

21. In Kabbalah and Chassidut the power of thought is considered to be the highest of the three "garments" of the psyche: thought, speech and action. In the *Tanya* (*Igeret Hakodesh*, ch. 22) we are taught that evil thoughts about someone are ultimately more harmful than speaking slander about him. It is therefore most important to guard the mind from impure thoughts and especially from evil thoughts about others as the Alter Rebbe pleads (*Igeret Hakodesh* ch. 22):

My beloved and dear ones, I beg again and again that each of you exert himself with all his heart and soul to firmly implant in his heart a love for his fellow Jew, and, in the words of Scripture, "Let none of you consider in your heart what is evil for his fellow" (Zachariah 8:17).

Moreover, [such a thought] should never arise in one's heart and if it does arise, one should push it away from his heart "as smoke is driven away" (Psalms 68:3), as if it were an actual idolatrous thought. For to speak evil [of another] is as grave as idolatry and incest and bloodshed (*Arachin* 15b). If this be so with speech, [then surely thinking evil about another is even worse]; for all the wise of heart are aware of the greater impact [on the soul] of thought over speech, whether for the good or for the better.

The phrase used by the sages in the Talmud that describes the power of thought is *machshavah moelet* (מחשבה מועלת; see *Zevachim* 13a), which has a negative connotation, since *moelet* is from the root meaning "sacrilege." However, *moelet* can also mean "effective," in which case this expression has a positive connotation, when thought effectively influences reality for the better.

22. The sixth Lubavitcher Rebbe, Rabbi Yosef Yitzchak Schneersohn, the Rayatz.

23. One example of the power of thought to positively affect a person is found in a letter sent by Rabbi Pinchas of Koritz to the Magid of Mezritch:

    Many thanks to his holy honor for mentioning me and thinking of me in his holy thoughts on Yom Kippur. His holy honor should know that the very moment I was privileged to arise in his holy memory, I immediately felt it in my ability to pray. (*Likutei Diburim*, 1.)

24. The sharp sight of the ostrich hen aids in hatching the chick, even without incubation (see *Etz Chayim* 8:1).

25. In the Talmud we find a classic description of such telepathic communication in the story of Job. The sages teach that, amazingly, Job's three friends felt Job's affliction from a distance of 300 *parsaot* (approximately 1,200 k.m.). They are considered true friends, so much so that at the end of the passage discussing this matter, Rava declares, "This is what people [mean when they] say, 'Either friends like those of Job, or death!'" (*Bava Batra*, 16b).

The Arizal stated that what delays the coming of the Mashiach is the lack of true heartfelt and soulful friendship—friends who are always connected to one another even by their thoughts.

26. *Hayom Yom*, 14th of *Shvat*.

27. *Keter Shem Tov* (Kehot edition, 1999), addendums 38 and 350.

LETTER 3

GIFTS FROM HEAVEN

I once heard a story about a tzadik *who was gifted with special spiritual powers but prayed to God that these powers be removed from him in order that he could serve God as a simple Jew.*

This seems to imply that Chassidut does not encourage the pursuit of spirituality and gaining spiritual powers. But, I don't understand why someone would want to return such a special God-given gift when God obviously intended it to be used for some purpose.

I would be grateful if you could please explain this to me.

INDEED, THERE ARE SEVERAL STORIES such as the one you mention in your letter, of great *tzadikim* who requested that certain spiritual powers be taken from them.[1]

A story that can shed light on your question is told of the Alter Rebbe, the spiritual "grandson"[2] of the Ba'al Shem Tov and the first Rebbe of Lubavitch. While on his way to his Rebbe, the Magid of Mezritch, he passed through the town of

Koritz, where Rebbe Pinchas of Koritz, another great disciple of the Ba'al Shem Tov, resided. After spending some time as a guest in Rebbe Pinchas' home, the Alter Rebbe wished to continue his journey to Mezritch. However, Rebbe Pinchas desired that he stay in Koritz and learn under his guidance.[3] In order to persuade him to stay, Rebbe Pinchas promised to teach him various forms of esoteric knowledge and practice, such as the ability to converse with angels, birds and trees. In spite of this apparently tempting offer, the Alter Rebbe remained steadfast in his decision to continue along his way to Mezritch. Regarding the spiritual gifts with which Rebbe Pinchas wished to bless him, he replied that in Mezritch these matters are of no particular interest. "In Mezritch we learn about 'the Single One', 'the One', and 'forever'" (three levels of Divine consciousness),[4] he said.[5] Later in his life, the Alter Rebbe said that all other matters of spirituality, such as those that Rebbe Pinchas offered to teach him, are mere technicalities that can be acquired and integrated into the psyche by the intelligent mind, with the one prerequisite that the student possesses Divine inspiration (*ruach hakodesh*), i.e. clarified Divine consciousness.

The prerequisite of *ruach hakodesh*, specified by the Alter Rebbe, is necessary for two reasons. First, *ruach hakodesh* is necessary in order to integrate the esoteric knowledge received through these techniques into one's psyche and thereby attain direct, sensory experience of the phenomena at hand, enabling correct interpretation of the perceived phenomenon. This is the literal meaning of the Alter Rebbe in his spiritual prescription. But this itself implies the second reason why *ruach hakodesh* is necessary, for without rectified *ruach hakodesh*, a person's apparent gifts, or acquired spiritual techniques, are unrectified as well,[6] possibly rendering his interpretation of the spiritual phenomenon he perceives of even less benefit than the rational advice of any well-meaning mentor.[7] Under such circumstances the person's spiritual gifts may become misleading and detrimental to himself and to others and they are most liable to disturb and disrupt his wholehearted and sincere service of God.

This is true of someone who is gifted with extraordinary spiritual senses (such as clairvoyance or healing powers), without having earned these gifts by devoted, humble service of God. "Earn" does not mean that he intends to receive them, but rather that, by his devoted service to come closer to God and fulfill His purpose in creation (in general and the purpose of his own existence in particular), he is given spiritual gifts that befit his spiritual level.[8]

However, someone who intends to receive such gifts through his service is considered a fool, as in the phrase, "A fool does not desire reason but the revelation of his heart."[9] A person deceives himself by believing that through his imagination and abstract thinking he is growing closer to understanding God. In fact, he is actually inflating his own ego. Even though he may indeed acquire certain "spiritual" powers, they are nothing more than a result of his own self-absorption. He thereby actually distances himself from achieving genuine spirituality.

Clearly, to possess such pseudo-spiritual powers is not one of the hallmarks of a truly righteous individual. The true seeker of God behaves with humility and selflessness and is always modest in his own eyes.

As explained at length in Rebbe Shneur Zalman's classic text, the *Tanya*, there are many levels of Divine service that a person must achieve on his way to becoming a *tzadik*. The more humility that the spiritually maturing person integrates into his psyche, the more likely he is to suspect that spiritual powers that he gained may be deceptive in nature, if he consciously worked to achieve them. In actual fact, these powers may be a test from Above intended to reveal the person's true desires. True spiritual powers are those that are gained unwittingly and in all innocence. Such a test distinguishes whether the person's goal is to experience spiritual powers that gratify his soul, or whether he is truly searching to unite with God, the Infinite One and Creator of the universe.[10]

So, it is important that we realize that spiritual powers are **not** necessarily a result of spiritual service, even with regard to the righteous (not to speak of the unrighteous who may also possess similar powers), but rather, such powers reflect innate qualities of the soul, as we will explain shortly. A pure, essentially righteous soul is one who is able to discern, in truth, whether the power he possesses brings him closer to the level of "direct communication with God" or not.

Let us clarify this point in greater depth, from a slightly different angle, beginning from the unrighteous and then returning to the righteous. Obviously, the vast majority of so-called "healers" and spiritual diviners etc. are nothing more than charlatans. This is true whether they deceive the public consciously or whether they themselves truly believe that they possess such powers.[11]

Yet there still exists a minute percentage of people who are truly capable of such divination, even without having purified themselves in holiness. Obviously though, these individuals certainly do not possess the prerequisite of *ruach hakodesh*.[12] Where do these powers emanate from? Why do some people possess them while others do not?

In order to explain this, we must first understand that the psyche of man has three garments; these are thought, speech and action, thought being the highest and the most important[13] of the three. An amazingly deep perception that Chassidut reveals is that the spiritual powers that certain people possess are the result of "holes" in the psychological garments that clothe the normative powers of their souls; a type of nakedness through which the light/energy rooted in the inner, super-conscious (or sub-conscious) powers of the soul leaks, as it were, into the conscious psyche.[14]

The sound integrity of the garments of the soul, is of utmost importance for one's psychological health. In fact, the Hebrew word for "rectification" (תיקון) is a synonym for "garment." Before the primordial sin, Adam and Eve were both naked and were not embarrassed of their nakedness. However, the rectification after the sin was to wear clothes. The sages teach us that the word for, "clothing" (לבוש) is a permutation of, "unembarrassed" (לא בוש), meaning that wearing clothing neutralizes the negative embarrassment that resulted from the sin. In the same way that clothing hides the blatant physicality of our bodies, allowing our inner personalities to become apparent when we interact with others, so too these three "layers" of spiritual clothing serve to hide-yet-reflect the innermost recesses of our spiritual being. So, just as torn clothing is generally something that we are embarrassed about, such holes are similarly undesirable.

Through their prayers, the *tzadikim* elevate and purify their garments, particularly the garment of thought.[15] The pure and refined garments then rise to clothe the inner powers of the soul,[16] now serving to channel super-conscious light/energy to the *tzadik* in a rectified manner. He receives new, rectified spiritual powers that others do not possess, and he is able to utilize them for the benefit of mankind as God truly desires.

Individuals whose spiritual powers are a result of the "holes" in their garments, are in fact born with a defect, just as a person may be born lacking a certain limb, God forbid. There are some limbs that are more crucial than others and a person is able to survive without that limb. Such a person may even develop increased sensitivity in another limb to overcome his disability. Similarly, someone born with "holes" in a particular spiritual garment may develop sharper insight than is normal, as well as spiritual "powers." For example, the sages of the

Talmud tell us that there are those who are born with the ability to interpret dreams (and their interpretation, indeed, comes true),[17] yet they need not be righteous souls at all; indeed the Talmud recounts tragic incidents wrought by evil dream-interpreters.[18]

In contrast, the true *tzadik*, who has been awarded special powers through his efforts to purify his soul, is able to selflessly assist those who turn to him for help. The special insight of the *tzadik* helps him see the particular point of rectification that the person approaching him needs, his help is thus focused on what that person needs in order to truly rectify himself.

Yet, even so, the heightened consciousness of the *tzadik* makes him aware of the spiritual anguish that the average person suffers as a result of his imperfect state. The *tzadik* may therefore experience even more pain than the person himself,[19] resulting in a certain existential frustration for the *tzadik*. Because of his true empathy with the suffering soul, his own

One of the disciples of the Seer of Lublin, like his master, was conscious of many things of which normal people were not aware. He was once asked to pray for the complete recovery of a sick man who was in dire danger, however he refused to do so. The man's family continued to plead with him that he pray that the man live, but the Rebbe continued to refuse. At last the Rebbe cried out, "How can you expect me to pray that this man live, when I know that there is a young woman in the next village who is suffering in a long drawn-out labor because this man must die in order that her child receive his soul in a new incarnation?! How can I pray that he live?!!" After this episode, the Rebbe pleaded to God to remove this spiritual power from him.

psychological suffering knows no end. Moreover, the *tzadik* is not always able to redeem the other soul from its spiritual exile and he remains absorbed in his own suffering, to no avail. The superconscious knowledge of the *tzadik* may make him aware of self-contradictory spiritual situations that prevent him from offering his assistance to those who request it.

Were the *tzadik* unaware of such paradoxical spiritual situations, he would be able to pray wholeheartedly and in all sincerity for Divine assistance for the person in trouble, leaving the solution of paradoxes entirely up to God, "the Paradox of all Paradoxes." Such a state of disharmony that results from their own ability to perceive beyond the limits of normal consciousness, is why the *tzadikim* prefer to serve God in the manner of a simple Jew whose prayers are innocent and guileless, having no awareness of the spiritual complexities of which the *tzadik* is aware.

From all that we have said above, this last scenario presents but one justification for the *tzadik* to ask God to take from him spiritual gifts.

Of greatest importance is to remember that the spiritual maturity necessary to assume and succeed in one's life's mission demands that one focuses his spiritual efforts on comprehending and integrating the levels of "the Single One," "the One," and "forever;" *yachid, echad, va'ed,* the curriculum that the Alter Rebbe studied in Mezritch.

With blessings of the Torah and the Land of Israel,

There was once a great and awe-inspiring king who erected many barriers, between each of which were many deep rivers and frightening military forces and bears and lions, snakes and scorpions and other wild animals, to scare away anyone who wished to approach the king. Each barrier and each juncture was more fearful than the last, so that nobody could come near without permission. The walls concealed the king and the wall that was closest to him was as dark as the plague of darkness in Egypt.

The king sent out heralds who announced that whoever arrived and received the privilege of seeing the king's face, would be entitled to gain the king's daughter as his bride, and a crown would be placed upon his head. He would rule over the whole of the king's kingdom, standing before him at all times and dwelling in his palace which was full of light.

Who is the fool who does not desire such a thing?! Yet, anyone who approaches the wall and sees such frightening and terrible things, tasting of the great bitterness that stems from his wish to come closer to the king, becomes discouraged. There are a few who, after overcoming great trials, succeed in penetrating a number of the walls, but between every wall they encounter many respected noblemen, who give out great wealth to whoever desires to stay with them there. Anyone wishing to persevere and continue on his way to see the king's countenance will have to encounter fearful and terrible things that embitter the soul and terrify him with fear and terror, and snakes and scorpions who try to prevent him from advancing to see the king's countenance. Sometimes, after he discovers that he can remain with the king's noblemen, and he has great wealth, he remains where he is, because each wall is ever higher and more threatening than the last.

Yet a true prince, who longs for his father's love, has no intention to receive personal benefit, but only wishes to do as his father, the king, desires. He is willing to endure anything that will enable him to receive audience with the king. When he approaches the fearful walls, the rivers, the military forces, the snakes and scorpions, and all the darkness that conceals the king's countenance, he is astonished why such a merciful king, who has mercy as a father has on his sons, should obscure himself behind such barriers? By power of his broken heart and his burning desire to be with his father, the prince completely devotes himself to the task with great self-sacrifice and accepts upon himself all the anguish he suffers with love. He perseveres with great strength and suffers many torments from the snakes and scorpions, bears and lions and frightening barriers. He discards all the wealth and acquisitions that he receives from the king's noblemen, not desiring them at all. With a joyful heart he leaps over the mountains and skips over the hills, until he is privileged to see the king, completely selfless, egoless and with a broken heart, with a fiery desire and a flaming love. When he finally sees the king, he begins to weep rivers of tears, "Why, o' merciful father?! I was almost lost because of the many barriers, the darkness and the bitterness and all the temptations that the noblemen dispensed in order to persuade me not to come before you!"

Then the king opens his eyes, saying, "Look outside and see that there is not one single barrier, there are no snakes and not one screen nor a single mask, for the light of the king's countenance shines from one end of the world to the other, and within all of the darkness and the bitterness, the king shines in all his glory."

Once the prince's eyes are opened, he sees that all of these terrifying things are there in order to bring him closer to the king; only a fool does not perceive this and he chooses to remain with the noblemen.

The king then gives his daughter to the prince, that is the power of prayer, to unite him with the king, and the power to decree death or life, to forbid and to permit, to raise and to lower, by the power of the light of the king's countenance that shines upon him.[20]

Notes:

1. For example, see story inset in Letter 1.

2. The greatest disciple of the Ba'al Shem Tov's greatest disciple, the Magid of Mezritch.

3. Every great *tzadik* has a passion to teach great, high souls, and none was like the Alter Rebbe in his generation. The story told here is a classic example of the application of the phrase, "More than the calf wishes to suckle, the cow wishes to nurse," which Rabbi Akiva said to Rabbi Shimon bar Yochai when he approached him to learn Torah (*Pesachim* 112a).

   By answering the perpetual questions of his students, the teacher is compelled to extend his knowledge to accommodate their needs. This is more taxing to his capabilities than even studying with a well-matched study partner or learning from a great Torah scholar, as the sages teach us, "I have learned much from my masters, I have learned more from my friends [study partners] and from my students I have learned more than all of them!" (*Ta'anit* 7a).

   In addition, in the teacher-student relationship, the teacher is relatively "male," infusing his more "female" student with wisdom and inspiration. The student takes the conceptual ideas and develops them, much as a fetus develops in his mother's womb, resulting in the "birth" of practical applications of which the teacher was perhaps unaware at the outset.

4. The absolute state of unity of God's very essence is referred to as *yachid*, "the single One," implying that there is no true existence other than God. "God is One [*echad*]" means that God permeates all of creation and that all of creation exists within Him, above time and space as we know them. *Va'ed*, "forever," implies that God's light and presence, His kingdom, permeate reality within the context of created time and space.

   In the two verses of the *Shema* proclamation (*Shema Yisrael... **echad*** and *Baruch Shem... le'olam **va'ed***), the verse of the *Shema*, referred to in the *Zohar* as "the higher union," expresses the unity of God at the second level of *echad*, "one" (the concluding word of the verse), the union of the world in God (while the level of *yachid*, "single one," is merely implied, in order to allow the revelation of God's unity in the context of creation, as explained in Chassidut). The word *va'ed*, "forever," which concludes the second verse, is referred to in the *Zohar* as "the lower union," the union of God in the world (see *Tanya, Sha'ar Hayichud Veha'emunah*, ch. 7).

The sum of the numerical values of *yachid* (יחיד) and *echad* (אחד) is 45, which is the numerical value of the word, "what" (מה) referring to the ultimate state of selflessness and humility, the non-existence of God's creations as separate entities, as Moses said of himself and his brother Aharon, "what are we?" (Exodus, 16:7; *ibid* v. 8)

Together with the numerical value of the word *va'ed* (ועד) the total value of the three words is 125, or 5^3. This alludes to the sages' interpretation of the verse "This is the history of the heavens and the earth *behibaram* [when they were created]," which the sages interpret to mean, *be'hei bera'am*, meaning that the world was created with the letter *hei*, which has a numerical value of 5. 5 to the power of three, therefore, refers to the letter *hei* on three levels: *yachid, echad,* and *va'ed.*

5. In a similar vein, after the passing of the Ba'al Shem Tov, his followers sat and related stories of the miraculous wonders that he had wrought in his lifetime. The Ba'al Shem Tov appeared to some of his students and said to them, "Why are you engaged in relating sensational acts? Tell about my fear of Heaven instead!" (see our book in Hebrew, *Or Yisrael*, Vol. 3, p. 73).

6. See in depth in our Hebrew book *Shechinah Beineihem* p. 35.

7. Even if the gifts have been earned, they may still be a test. Spiritual gifts of this nature should be retained only if they have been truly earned. Such gifts must also assist a person in his Divine service to reach his Father, thus, ultimately, bringing rectification and redemption to the world.

8. See also the parable in frame, above.

9. Proverbs 18:2.

10. Indeed, the universe is none but a reflection of God's knowledge of Himself, and thus, ultimately, God is all and all is God (see *Mishneh Torah, Hilchot Yesodei Hatorah*, 1:1).

11. As the sixth Lubavitcher Rebbe once said, the entire *Tanya*, the classic text of Chassidut, is intended to save people from self-deception.

12. The spiritual powers possessed by those with psychic holes are chaotic in nature (in the terminology of Kabbalah, they derive from the World of Chaos). Chaotic phenomena are always accompanied by arrogance, whether fully conscious or partially unconscious. This, of course, renders the advice or therapy that one receives from such people counterproductive. The wise will surely keep their distance from them!

13. In Hebrew, the word for, "important" (חשוב) even shares the same root with the word for, "thought" (מחשבה).

14. This is in accord with the saying of the sages that since the destruction of the Temple in Jerusalem, prophecy has been taken from the prophets and given to fools and children (*Bava Batra* 12b). The common denominator between fools and children is that they lack the faculty of *da'at*, which serves to filter out the superconscious knowledge that enters the mind of the average person, allowing only rational thoughts to pass through. In the rectified mind of the righteous, the faculty of *da'at* is clarified to such an extent that even such superconscious knowledge can be analyzed and integrated by his psyche, without affecting him adversely.

15. In Kabbalah and Chassidut the power of thought is considered to be the highest of the three garments of the soul: thought, speech and action. It is therefore most important to guard the mind from impure thoughts and from evil thoughts about others. In a certain sense evil thoughts about someone are even more damaging than speaking slander about him or actually taking harmful physical action against him (*Tanya, Igeret Hakodesh*, ch. 22).

16. The next two powers of the soul above these three are called "emotions" (מידות) and "intellect" (שכל). Emotions are "pathos" or

feelings, while the intellect is pure, abstract intellect that is isolated from feelings. The Alter Rebbe, author of the *Tanya*, explains that whereas thought, speech and action are garments, which can be changed and renewed with ease, the emotions and intellect are the essential powers of the soul. The inner, abstract light of the intellect can be harnessed and utilized by the garment of thought when, through its purification and clarification, the power of thought rises to clothe the pure intellect. For more about these levels of the soul's faculties, see *Anatomy of the Soul*.

17. See *Tosafot* on *Berachot* 55b.

18. The Talmud relates that once two sages dreamt exactly the same dream and went to the same dream interpreter. One of the sages gave the interpreter a coin, while the other did not. The interpreter positively interpreted the dream of the sage who paid him and his interpretation proved true, while to the sage who did not pay he offered a bad interpretation which unfortunately, also came true (*ibid.*, 56a).

19. God's great compassion encompasses all of creation, from the very highest spiritual levels of creation down to our physical reality. Only God knows the great extent of His compassion on us, infinitely more than we can know with regard to ourselves. In this respect, the *tzadik*'s own compassion for the sufferer reflects that of God.

20. There are a number of versions to this parable, we have brought here the version that appears in *Heichal Habrachah*. See also our book in Hebrew, *Be'itah Achishenah* pp. 151-153.

Letter 4

Glowing Letters

I dreamt that I was awakened in the middle of the night and saw that all the walls in my room, the chair, the desk — everything — was made of glowing Hebrew letters. The walls were not regular material anymore, they were all made of glowing Hebrew letters. It was a very realistic dream. When I tried to touch the letters, I woke up. That is all I can remember.
Could you please tell me what this dream is trying to say.

Your dream is most meaningful. Indeed, meditation on the fact that everything in the world is made of Hebrew letters is one of the most central focuses of Kabbalah and Chassidut.[1]

The Hebrew letters, especially those contained in the Ten Sayings that God spoke at the outset of creation,[2] together with their innumerable permutations and transformations, are channels of Divine consciousness, energy and life-force, by which God created and continuously recreates everything, as explained in Chassidut.[3]

In a certain sense, the Hebrew letters, the building blocks of the universe, can be seen to vitalize reality much as the encoded "letters" of DNA build and define the form and function of the human body. Indeed, the twenty-two Hebrew letters are reflected in the number of chromosomes in human seed. The twenty-two male chromosomes together with the twenty-two female chromosomes define forty-four characteristics of the human offspring, the secret of the Hebrew word for "blood" (דם, which has a numerical value of 44). Together, the parents' two sex chromosomes define a single characteristic of the offspring—its gender. This is reflected in the letter *alef* (א), which has a numerical value of 1. The form of the *alef* (י above, י below, both connected by a ו) portrays the male sex chromosome and the female sex chromosome uniting to become one. In the word אדם, meaning "man," the letter א precedes the letters of the word דם.

Similarly, the various proteins that compile the basic structure of every cell in the human body are made up of twenty-two amino acids (twenty standard and two non-standard). Thus from these two physiological examples, we can begin to see how the twenty-two Hebrew letters lie at the foundation of all created matter.

The word for "letter" in Hebrew (אות) also means "sign" or "wonder." It is also the word used to refer to "the sign of the covenant," the circumcision, which is stamped on the body of every Jewish male on the eighth day after birth.[4] In *Sefer Yetzirah*, the twenty-two letters are called "the twenty-two letters of [the *sefirah* of] foundation." In Kabbalah, the power of foundation relates to the sign of circumcision which, when guarded in sanctity, serves as the key to opening the secret teachings of the Hebrew letters, enabling them to enter the consciousness of one's mind and heart.[5]

The *sefirah* of foundation represents the power of the soul to relate and connect to other souls and beings. By being connected to each letter of the Torah one obtains the power to productively relate and connect to every soul of Israel.

The letters of the Hebrew word for "Israel" (ישראל), are the initial letters of the phrase, "There are six-hundred thousand letters in the Torah."[6] Six hundred thousand is also the number of the Children of Israel who were released from the Egyptian bondage,[7] signifying that this number is the core number of souls of the Jewish people. This indicates that each Jewish soul is connected to one letter of the Torah, and by connecting to each and every letter of the Torah, a person connects to all the souls of the entire Jewish people.[8]

Similarly, by creating genuine, loving relationships towards one's friends, one strengthens his bond to the letters of the Torah.

Most obviously, the twenty-two Hebrew letters also form the basis of language, the most universal means of communication amongst humans. But, although this may be less apparent, the letters actually exist at various levels of energy even during the processes that precede the formation of words, as we shall see.

The individual letters of a word represent the state of the initial, relatively amorphous thought that entered the person's mind before he actually formed the thought into words. They contain the potential meaning, the latent energy from which the actual meaning of the word is composed.

Once words begin to form in the mind, the letters within the words channel the life-force (from the lights, the *sefirot*) that vitalizes the yet unspoken words.

The speaker then constructs his particular style of expression by his choice of words. At this level, the letters become the inspiration that illuminates the essence of the spoken idea, reflecting the initial amorphous thought.

The fact that the letters that you saw were glowing indicates that the lights (the *sefirot*) were present within the vessels (the letters), suggesting a state of completion in which the initial idea is apparent within the spoken word.

As the letters evolve into speech and become constrained in the words that are formed, their abstract energy level contracts considerably.[9] This idea allows us to gain an infinitesimal glimpse into the infinite Divine wisdom contained within the Hebrew letters in the following manner: first we contemplate the energy level and life-force of God's spoken word at work in the creation of the universe. The energy in one such spoken word is greater than all the physical and spiritual energy that we can ever fathom. But then we compare this to the energy level of God's hidden word, His thought, as it were. Next, we contemplate that God's thought reflects His wisdom, the wisdom of the Torah, which itself possesses two levels: the revealed level of the Torah, the revelation of God's will to man, and the concealed level of the Torah, the unknowable "reasons" behind the Divine will. The energy level of God's revealed will is naught, as it were, in comparison to the energy level of the inner mysteries of the Torah. The true origin of the Hebrew letters lies at this highest energy level of Divine wisdom, and so, although infinitely beyond the scope of human intellect,[10] studying and meditating on the Hebrew letters is the limit to which our minds are capable of perceiving God's majesty.

Since the act of touching entails an involvement of the self and the ego, your inability to touch the letters you saw in your dream signifies that they can only be experienced in a state of true selflessness, the inner trait of the *sefirah* of wisdom. This phenomenon is similar to the finding in modern physics that contact by the observer, or even the mere act of observation, influences or changes the phenomenon observed and may even make it disappear. The spark of wisdom and inspiration necessary to enable "touching" or experiencing the phenomenon of the Hebrew letters is only able to enter our psyches when we nullify our egos.

This idea is expressed by the following story:

A short time before his passing, Rabbi Shneur Zalman of Liadi (the first Rebbe of Chabad), lying in bed, pointed at the ceiling and asked his grandson (Rabbi Menachem Mendel, the third Rebbe of Chabad) to tell him what he saw there. The young man answered that he saw the beams that held up the roof. The Alter Rebbe then replied, "Believe me when I tell you that I do not see the ceiling, I see only the Divine energy that creates it!"

In a similar vein, Rebbe Nachman of Breslov told an incredible story about a man who saw the letters that vitalized the food that he ate, later becoming the letters of the words of the Torah that he spoke.[11] Seeing the letters of the food one consumes is the first and foremost place to witness the letters of creation, as indicated in the verse, "Man does not live by bread alone, but by all that emanates from the mouth of God does man live."[12] The expression "all that emanates from the mouth of God" refers to the constant vitalization of every aspect of creation by the power of the Ten Sayings that God spoke during the six days of creation.[13]

Even though he may not be aware of it, a person derives his vital energy by ingesting the letters,[14] the vessels which contain the Divine lights, or energies, of creation. This idea is beautifully illustrated by the custom of celebrating the first time a child is taught to read. During the ceremony, the child is allowed to lick honey from a slate on which the Hebrew letters are written. In this way, his inauguration into the world of letters is a sweet experience, and the sweetness of the letters makes a lasting impression upon the child.

The fact that you dreamt that you were awakened in the middle of the night relates to the time of *tikun chatzot*, the prayer recited at midnight, mourning the destruction of the Temple. Seeing glowing letters at that time alludes to the rebuilding of the Temple, which will herald the ultimate rectification of the consciousness of all reality that is condensed within its confines. This consciousness is the ability to perceive the continual influx of the Divine letters of creation and of the Torah in all aspects of our lives.

With blessings of the Torah and the Land of Israel,

Notes:

1. In a letter to his brother-in-law, Rabbi Gershon of Kitov, the Ba'al Shem Tov wrote, "In every letter there are Worlds, Souls and Divinity, and they ascend and connect and unify with each other, and afterward the letters connect and unify to become a word, and [then] unify in true unification in Divinity. Include your soul with them in each and every state." For an in-depth discussion of the meanings of the Hebrew letters, see our book, *The Hebrew Letters: Channels of Creative Consciousness.*

2. See Letter 12, note 9.

3. *Tanya, Sha'ar Hayichud Ve'haemunah*, ch. 1.

4. A Jewish female is considered to be "born circumcised" (*Avodah Zara* 27a), possessing the "holy sign" within herself from the moment of birth.

5. It is strongly recommended that you study our book, *The Hebrew Letters: Channels of Divine Consciousness*, which greatly expands on the ideas mentioned above.

   It would also be advisable for you to study the second section of the *Tanya*, in which the topic of the Hebrew letters and their function in creation is discussed in depth. There, the Alter Rebbe (the first Rebbe of Lubavitch) explains that the twenty-two letters of the Hebrew *alef-bet* correspond to the origin of the vessels, that hold the lights of the ten supernal *sefirot*.

   In order to visualize the relation between the numbers 10 and 22 [i.e., how 22 (letters) contain 10 (*sefirot*)], think of a strip of material 1 unit wide by 10 units long. The perimeter of this strip is 22 (one-dimensional) units, and contains an area of 10 (two-dimensional) units.

Another mathematical relationship between the two numbers 10 and 22 is that the volume of a 3 dimensional triangle (tetrahedron) of 10 units [which is equal to the sum of all triangles from the triangle of 1 (1), to the triangle of 10 (55)] is equal to 220 (cubic units), or 10 times 22. Each of the four faces of such a tetrahedron is itself a triangle with a base of 10 units (area of 55 square units), so its surface area is also 220 (square units).

6. *Megaleh Amukot*, 186.

7. Exodus, 12:37.

8. *Tanya*, ch. 37. We are further taught that, like all that is holy, the Hebrew letters possess the property of inter-inclusion: i.e., every letter contains (is able to reflect from within itself) all of the letters. Each of the six hundred thousand letters of the Torah is thus a gateway to the entire Torah, for each letter contains all of the letters. (See *Tanya, Igeret Hateshuvah* ch. 4; *Tanya, Sha'ar Hayichud Veha'emunah,* ch. 11.) Indeed, if even one letter is missing from a Torah scroll, the entire scroll is disqualified for use until it is corrected. Likewise, every one of the six hundred thousand soul-roots of Israel possesses six hundred thousand sparks, each spark being capable of giving life to an individual body.

9. See *Tanya, Sha'ar Hayichud Veha'emunah* ch. 9.

10. As the verse states, "Your thoughts are not My thoughts" (Isaiah 55:8); see also *Tanya*, ch. 21.

11. See story at end of *Peulat Hatzadik*.

12. Deuteronomy 8:3. Similarly, the Torah, the revelation of God's essence, constructed from the Hebrew letters, is referred to as "bread" (Proverbs 9:5).

13. The numerical value of the phrase "that emanates from the mouth of God" (מוצא פי הוי') equals 253 which is the triangle of 22 (the sum of all

integers from 1 to 22), alluding to the twenty-two letters of the Hebrew language which vitalize the world.

14. The most basic blessing recited over food is "Blessed are You, God… that all came into being by His word."

The foremost composition of the *mesorah* (notes on Biblical tradition, initiated in order to prevent inadvertent changes to the Bibilical text), entitled "*Ochlah Ve'Ochlah,*" is named after the very first entry in its list of words. From here we can deduce that the most elementary root in Hebrew is אכל meaning "to eat." Although alphabetically this is not the first root in the Hebrew language, the reduced numerical values of the three letters of this root are 1, 2 and 3, expressing the most primary series of addition.

By breaking the root אכל into each of its two syllables, א-כל we can begin to understand its importance, as it refers to the one God [the letter *alef* (א) has a numerical value of 1. Also, the name of the letter (אלף) refers to "the Master of the World" (אלופו של עולם)] who is "all" (כל; and all is One). Thus, eating is the action which, ideally, is most capable of filling our consciousness with the absolute unity of God.

LETTER 5

ANGEL OF DREAMS

A friend of mine told me that you can interpret dreams. I therefore ask for an interpretation for this dream that I had a few months ago. The following is all I can remember about the dream:

I'm sitting at a table in a room in a house. All I recall seeing is a girl of approximately eighteen years old. She has blond, straight hair that falls to just below, and covering, her ears. She is wearing a dress that is a mix of earthy colors. However, I can't remember what colors specifically anymore. My view of her and the room and table disappear briefly and filling my vision are the letters mem, lamed, chaf, alef. *Upon seeing these letters I transpose them in my mind, and I think that the word must be* malach, *meaning "angel." The letters disappear and the view of the girl at the table, etc. returns. I ask the girl in my dream if she is an angel. At this point, I wake up.*

Here ends the dream. The story continues, however. I go to synagogue, it is Shabbat morning, and during the Torah portion the word melachah *[meaning "work"] is read and I realize that* melachah *contains all the letters of the word in my dream, with the addition of the letter* hei. *Ever since then I have been completely confused as to what the word I saw in my dream meant and who the girl in my dream was. I asked a few people if they knew of any Hebrew words spelled* mem, lamed, chaf, alef, *but they did not know any. I'm writing hoping that you will be able to tell me what my incomprehensible-to-me dream means.*

ALTHOUGH the general rule is that "dreams speak in vain,"[1] implying that we should not become obsessed with our dreams nor take them too seriously, sometimes the symbols contained in dreams can be meaningful and help direct us in our service of God. However, even while attempting to interpret a dream that seems to be of significance, one should take into account that "there is no dream without idle images,"[2] meaning that not all of the details of the dream require intensive contemplation.

Obviously, the most significant symbols that one can see in a dream are Hebrew letters,[3] especially when they combine to form a meaningful word or statement, such as in the case of your dream.[4]

Indeed, as you thought, the Hebrew letters you saw in your dream can be arranged to spell the word meaning "angel"

(מלאך). Or, variably, they can be arranged to spell the word meaning "food" (מאכל). Interestingly, Rebbe Nachman of Breslov mentions two types of dreams, which correspond to each of these permutations: a) dreams that are produced by the chemical and spiritual effects of the foods that we eat (מאכל); b) dreams that are brought on by angels (מלאך).

Food: "Not by bread alone shall man live but by all that issues from the mouth of God shall man live".[6] Kabbalah and Chassidut explain that this verse teaches us that the sustenance we receive from food is

> The total numerical value of these four letters is 91, which is a very important number in Kabbalah. This is the combined value of the two Divine Names, Havayah (26)—God's essential Name which is forbidden to pronounce as written—and Adni (65), the way that the Name Havayah is pronounced. The Name Havayah represents God's transcendence, while the Name Adni represents God's immanence, thus when combined, the two Names together express God's paradoxical ability to transcend and "surround" all worlds, while simultaneously being immanent and "within" all worlds.[5]

actually from the energy of the letters that issued from God's words during creation and that continues to determine the existence of creation at every single moment. The numerical value of the phrase, "That which issues from the mouth of God" (מוצא פי הוי'), is 253, which is the sum of all integers from 1 to 22. This alludes to the fact that the twenty-two Hebrew letters which God uttered in order to create the world lie at the core of all physical matter. Thus, the food that we ingest is, in fact, the physical manifestation of the particular combination of Hebrew letters that brings it into existence, and that provides its life-energy to sustain us.

When we dream at this level, our consciousness rises to the energy level of the letters with which God sustains the existence of the foods that we eat.[7]

Angel: The type of dream that a person dreams depends on the extent to which he has clarified his mind. If he clarifies his mind from all negative thoughts, in particular from thoughts of adultery, then his dreams appear to him via an angel. However, if, God forbid, his thoughts are not clarified, then his dreams appear via an evil spirit.

In the order that you saw them, these letters spell the Aramaic for "the king" (מלכא) as in the phrase referring to Mashiach (מלכא משיחא).

The word Hebrew word meaning, "work" or "craft" (מלאכה) is actually the feminine form of "angel."[8] An angel is a messenger sent by God to perform a certain task or action. The Torah defines thirty-nine categories of craft that are forbidden to do on Shabbat, the day of rest.[9] These were the thirty-nine crafts necessary for the construction of the Tabernacle (which, in Jewish law does not supersede the mandatory rest of Shabbat[10]). Each category is a form of rectification, as the sages teach us that the root meaning "to do" (עשה)[11] also means, "to rectify."[12] God created the world in a way that allows mankind to take part in the creation process. Through our actions, God's plan in creation is brought to completion.

Indeed, the constructive work, those rectifications that we accomplish during the week, is brought to life on Shabbat in the image of a bride[13] or the "Shabbat Queen,"[14] as we acknolwedge God's supremacy over all that we accomplish during the week by refraining from those forbidden crafts on Shabbat. This is beautifully illustrated by the numerical value of Shabbat (שבת), which is 702, the product of 18 (the value of חי, meaning "life") and 39 (the categories of craft or rectification.)

We hope we have said enough to whet your imagination and inspire you to do your utmost to rectify reality throughout the week and rest and enjoy the Shabbat,[15] becoming one with God the Creator as He delights in the Torah and the souls of Israel before creation.[16]

With blessings of the Torah and the Land of Israel,

Notes:

1. Zachariah, 10:2. See also Letter 5, note 1; Letter 7, note 11; Letter 11, note 1; Letter 13, note 1.

2. *Berachot*, 55a. In general, the images one sees in dreams are reflections of the idle thoughts one has during the day (*ibid*, 55b). Since even a great *tzadik*, one who clings to God in mind and heart, is not totally free of idle thought, so too, even a true dream, such as the dreams of the righteous Joseph, must contain a certain amount of idle images (*ibid*, 55a).

3. The Torah letters are the building blocks of the universe. Each of the twenty-two Hebrew letters is a channel connecting the Infinite with the finite. The name, form and number of each letter express its individual manner of transforming energy into matter, by

contracting the infinite spiritual light and life force into a finite letter. This can be compared to the relationship between the phenomena of thought and speech in the soul. The spiritual state before the appearance of the letter is like a thought, as yet unexpressed. The letter itself is like the expression of the thought through speech, which, while expressing the thought, also constricts it and transforms it into accessible material (for more about the significance of the Hebrew letters as the building blocks of creation, see the introduction to *The Hebrew Letters*).

Before God's letters of creation combine into words, they are still unable to give life to individual creatures. In this inanimate state they are called "stones" (see *Sefer Yetzirah*, chapter 4:12). When the stones are combined into words, the "houses" thereby constructed receive power to give life even to physical creatures. Thus, the inner life of every creature is its Hebrew name (see *Tanya, Sha'ar Hayichud Veha'emunah*, chs. 1 and 12). See also Letter 14, note 19, below.

4. The Talmud (*Berachot* 55b) states that one should wait for a good dream to materialize for up to twenty-two years. Rabbi A. Y. Kook explains that each year represents the complete revelation of one of the twenty-two letters of the *alef-bet* and, with the completion of twenty-two years, the idea expressed in a dream reaches maturity and completion (*Ein Ayah*, p. 268, par. 41).

5. The number 91 is also the numerical value of the word *amen* (אמן), the expression of faith and truth that we reply after hearing a prayer or a blessing. The word *amen* expresses the union of these two Names of God. The sages therefore state that, "One who answers, '*amen*' [after hearing a blessing] is greater than one who makes a blessing" (*Berachot* 53b). One who makes a blessing is only able to articulate the Name *Adni*, while the Name *Havayah* is present only in his inner intention, his inner voice [*Tikunei Zohar*, intro. (3a)]. One who answers "*Amen!*" has, in fact united both Names into one articulated word.

Furthermore, 91 is also the product of 7 and 13, which signifies the perfect union of reality's male dimension, represented by the number 13, and its female dimension, represented by the number 7.

91 is also the sum of all integers from 1 to 13 (also called "the triangle of 13"), indicating the consummate state of Divine unity from 1 to *echad* (אחד, meaning "one," has a numerical value of 13), in love [the Hebrew word for "love" (אהבה) also has a numerical value of 13].

6. Deuteronomy 8:3.

7. *Likutei Moharan* I, 19:9; *Likutei Moharan* II, 1:6-7 and 5:10.

8. See *Sefer Hashorashim Laradak* (לא״כ).

9. The Hebrew phrase used in the Mishnah (*Shabbat* 7:2) to refer to the thirty-nine types of craft is, "forty minus one" (ארבעים חסר אחת). In Hebrew, this phrase has a numerical value of 1000 (the sum of the initial letters of each word in the phrase equals 10, the third root of 1000), which alludes to the one thousand lights that were given to Moses on Mt. Sinai, the consummate consciousness of "one" (1000 "reduces" to 1, i.e., it consummately reflects 1, as indicated by the fact that the name of the first letter of the Hebrew alphabet, *alef*, whose numerical value is 1, can also mean *elef*, "one thousand"). These lights were taken from Moses when the Jewish nation sinned with the golden calf. However, every Shabbat they are returned to him (and to the spark of his soul present within every Jew). This is because the rectification of the sin of the golden calf was to build the Tabernacle by means of the thirty-nine types of labor or craftsmanship. On Shabbat these one thousand lights are returned to Moses (and us) as reward for laboring at the forty-minus-one different types of craft during the week and refraining from them on Shabbat (that is to say that the "missing" one from the forty was indeed latently present within the weekday service of rectification by means of physical labor, and on Shabbat, the day of rest, becomes revealed in full).

10. The verses forbidding labor on the Shabbat are juxtaposed to the verses referring to the building of the Tabernacle, from which the

sages learn that it is specifically the types of labor that were necessary for building the Tabernacle that are forbidden on the Shabbat (see Exodus ch. 31; *Shabbat* 49b).

11. "Six days shall you work and you shall do all of your labor but on the seventh, Shabbat for GOD your God" (Exodus 20:8-9).

12. Rashi to Genesis 1:7.

13. *Shabbat* 119a. The word for "bride" in Hebrew (כלה) shares the same root as the words used to describe God's completion of the act of creation (ויכל) and His abstention from further acts on the seventh day (ויכל). Genesis 2:1-2.

14. *Shabbat,* 119a; *Tikunei Zohar,* intro. (2a).

15. Shabbat is the day for experiencing spiritual pleasure, as stated in the Book of Isaiah, "and you shall call the Shabbat pleasure..." (Isaiah 58:13-14; see *Metzudat David* to this verse). The Divine light revealed on Shabbat is referred to in Kabbalah as the light of *Abba* (the "father" principle), which contains three lines of loving-kindness (right), might (left) and beauty (middle). In our experience of Shabbat these three correspond to pleasure, refraining from work and rest, respectively. Refraining from work on Shabbat (בטול מלאכה) implies a consciousness of selflessness (בטול), whereas rest (מנוחה) is the united consciousness of pleasure and selflessness.

16. This is the level at which God rejoiced, as it were, in His creations before their creation. In Kabbalah, this level is referred to as, "essential recreation" (שעשועים עצמיים). (See *Emek Hamelech, Sha'ar Sha'ashuim Atzmi'im.*)

LETTER 6

A SYMBOL OF LIFE

As I go to bed at night and reach a state of relaxation (still very much awake), I start seeing faces of people. They stand and walk around in a place that is not bright with light, nor dark, just shadowed. Some of them look at me; I know they see me as I see them. Some are at peace, and some are very frightened. The frightened ones are taken away by a dark figure, while the peaceful are met by a beautiful man in white, whose face is featured but not detailed. I see the symbol "ת" over and over.

Is there some kind of meaning in this? If so, I am hoping that you could be gracious and help. I have talked to many people who think that I am weird, but I know that these people who I see are not my imagination.

I am not of the Jewish faith, but I am faithful and love God with all my heart. I am not afraid of what I see; I am only disturbed because I don't know what the meaning of this might be. I searched until I finally found the symbol I see, but all I know about it is that it is used in the Torah.

*Please do not think badly of me, I really would like
to find out. I am sincere. Thank you.*

THE SYMBOL THAT YOU MENTION is the Hebrew letter ת (*tav*).
This is the twenty-second and final letter of the Hebrew
alphabet. The name of the letter means "a mark" or "a
symbol."

In the Book of Ezekiel, a man[1] is commanded to put a mark
on the foreheads of the righteous people of Jerusalem who will
be saved from death; he is then commanded to kill the wicked.[2]

The sages in the Talmud explain that in fact both the righteous
and the wicked had a *tav* marked on their forehead. The
righteous people had a *tav* of ink on their forehead, while the
sinners had a *tav* of blood on their forehead. The letter *tav*
symbolized either *tichyeh* (meaning "live!") or *tamut*
(meaning "die!").

For the righteous, the *tav* of ink meant

The numerical value of the word meaning, "die!" (תמות) is equal to exactly twice the numerical value of the word meaning, "live!" (תחיה). This is in keeping with the rule of "a whole [846] and another half [423]," indicating that someone who has transgressed and is fated to death, must redouble his efforts to change his ways by returning wholeheartedly to God and also by giving an abundance of charity.[3] In this way, "die!" is transformed to become a double blessing of life (in this world and in the World to Come).[4]

Another beautiful example of "a whole and another half" is Havayah (26) echad (13), "GOD is one." Together, 26 and 13 equal 39, which is the numerical value of the word "dew" (טל), the dew of rejuvenation and the dew of resurrection.[5]

that they had fulfilled the entire Torah from *alef*, the first letter of the Hebrew alphabet, to *tav*, the final letter (i.e., they had observed all that is written in the Torah as inscribed in ink on the parchment of the Torah scroll). For the wicked, the *tav* of blood meant that they had transgressed the entire Torah from *alef* to *tav* (and so had defiled or "killed" the letters themselves, shedding their blood, as it were).[6]

You are obviously a spiritual person, and it would be most advisable for you to draw near to the path of the Torah, and to identify with the truth as a "righteous gentile" who follows the Seven Laws of Noah given by God to all of mankind.[7]

It is very important that you pray solely to the God of Israel that He save all of humanity and bring the Mashiach to the world, so that all souls may be rectified.[8] Strive to be an even more honest, better and more generous person, and to spread the light of the Torah to all those with who you come into contact. The closer you come to your Creator and His ways, the more you will understand how to help others and inspire them as well. In this way, you yourself may be instrumental in nullifying or "sweetening" evil decrees.

To sweeten evil decrees one must be joyful in spirit.[9] Joy comes from our experience of knowing that we are not alone in this life. God is always with us and always looking over us with love and kindness, as a father who cares for his children.

Song and dance, as external manifestations of true joy, are particularly conducive to sweetening evil decrees.[10] In modern Hebrew, the word for a musical note is also *tav*, like the name of the letter. Seeing the symbol ת over and over is thus like seeing a musical score.

In Chassidut, we are taught that joyful and sad souls combine as notes of a collective melody of longing for God and redemption.[11] We are further taught that there is nothing more powerful than music.[12] Indeed, ת is the final letter of the Hebrew alphabet, signifying the final limit of words and speech, approaching silence. Similarly, music and song are a mode of expression that is above speech and beyond silence. In fact the power of music is so intense that we are taught that it has the potential to enliven the dead[13] as well as to do the opposite.

Try to learn some simple Chassidic meditative melodies and to integrate them into your very being. This will offer you the inspiration you need to project the spirit of life and goodness to the souls who appear to you.[14]

With blessings of the Torah and the Land of Israel,

Notes:

1. Ezekiel 9:4-11. In the Talmud (*Shabbat* 55a), the "man" in the prophecy of Ezekiel is identified as the angel Gabriel. Gabriel (גבריאל) is the angel of might and judgment (גבורה). In Kabbalah, we are taught that the heavenly court is located within the domain of the *sefirah* of might (גבורה), thus Gabriel is the appropriate emissary of God to distinguish the righteous from the evil and to mark them with the symbol. The numerical value of גבריאל (246) equals the phrase,"the image of God," (צלם א־להים), in which man was created. Gabriel represents the spiritual sensitivity to the revealed presence of

the Divine image in man, i.e. the extent that an individual lives in accordance with the Torah.

2. In the text of the verses cited in the previous note, the root תו appears three times: והתוית, תו and התו. These correspond to the three essential services of the soul that begin with the letter ת: repentance (תשובה), prayer (תפלה) and Torah study (תורה), which further correspond to the three patriarchs, Abraham, Isaac and Jacob, respectively. See also Letter 12, note 7.

For more on the letter *tav*, see *The Hebrew Letters*, pp. 323-327.

3. See *Tanya, Igeret Hateshuvah*.

4. In Kabbalah, this is the secret of the two nostrils of "the Long Countenance" (the source of infinite good and forgiveness). Life emanates from the right nostril and "life of life," that is granted to true penitents, emanates from the left nostril. The Mashiach is the ultimate manifestation of the breath of both nostrils (see note 8 below), the complete revelation of a whole together with another half.

Because of this greater gift of "life of life" that is granted to penitents (*ba'alei teshuvah*), the sages teach that the righteous are not capable of standing in the place where *ba'alei teshuvah* stand (*Berachot* 34b). Nonetheless, the Mashiach will ultimately succeed in causing even the righteous to earn the title of *ba'alei teshuvah* (*Zohar III*, 153b).

5. Isaiah 26:19.

6. *Shabbat* 55a.

7. For more on this subject, see *Kabbalah and Meditation for the Nations*.

8. "For I shall not battle forever, nor shall I be furious for eternity, because a spirit from before Me shall enwrap and souls have I made [rectified]" (Isaiah 57:16). The spirit that is mentioned in this verse is the Mashiach himself who is called "the spirit of our nostrils" (Lamentations 4:20). His Divine inspiration, in the form of prayer, will subdue and "enclothe" the whole of humanity causing them to

return to a state of purity and their souls to be rectified (*Likutei Moharan* I, 2:1).

9. See Letter 1, note 18 above.

10. *Likutei Moharan* I, 10:1 and elsewhere.

11. Rabbi Shneur Zalman of Liadi, *Torah Or, Miketz* 37d.

12. *Torah Or, Ki Tissa* 113b; *Likutei Moharan* I, 64:5.

13. We are taught that the source in the Torah for the resurrection of the dead is in the phrase, "Then Moses will sing" (*Sanhedrin* 91a).

14. The sages teach us that, in fact, all of the people of Jerusalem were marked for death, and they report a harsh debate between God and the attribute of judgment: "God said to Gabriel, 'Go and mark on the foreheads of the righteous a sign of ink so that the angels of destruction shall not overcome them, and upon the foreheads of the wicked a sign of blood so that the angels of destruction shall overcome them.' The attribute of judgment said to God, 'Master of the Universe, what is the difference between these and those?' God answered, 'These are completely righteous, and those are completely wicked.' She [the attribute of judgment] replied, 'They [the righteous] had the power to rebuke and they did not rebuke!' God said, 'It is revealed and known to Me that had they rebuked them, they [the wicked] would not have accepted it from them.' [The attribute of judgment] then replied, 'To You it is clear and known but to whom among them is it known?'" (*Shabbat* 55a). With this triumphant statement, the attribute of judgment succeeded, for the only time in history, in reversing a good decree to save the righteous into a stringent decree against them. We learn from here that we all have a responsibility for the spiritual wellbeing of our peers.

For Jews, this responsibility towards one's friends is a positive commandment that we are obligated to observe, "Someone who sees his friend sinning, or even acting in an inappropriate manner, it is a *mitzvah* for him to return him for the better and to instruct him that he is sinning… as it says, 'You shall surely rebuke your comrade'

(Leviticus 19:17)" (Rabbi Shneur Zalman of Liadi, *Shulchan Aruch Harav, Orach Chaim* 156:7).

Even though you are a non-Jew, nonetheless, as a righteous gentile you too should be very concerned for the physical and spiritual welfare of your peers, especially the welfare of those who appear to you (via your own subconscious, which is linked to the collective subconscious pool of souls, by God), as "One who is not commanded to do so, yet observes [the commandment]" (see *Kidushin* 31a; please note that only Jews, who are commanded to do so, are punishable for not giving rebuke when applicable). By expressing your concern for the welfare of your peers in this way, bringing them closer to the true belief in the God of Israel, you will also become closer to the true altruism identified with the soul of Israel and thereby you may even be inspired to convert to Judaism (see *Kabbalah and Meditation for the Nations* ch. 3).

LETTER 7

FEAR OF EVIL

I am involved in a legal situation with my stepmother. Ever since I requested a hearing from the courts, I have been experiencing strange things.

Last night I had a horrifying nightmare where I felt that some terrible "thing" was trying to get at me. I cannot even express to you the terror I felt last night. I awoke screaming and when I finally composed myself I began to recite the **Shema** *over and over and over, until the prayer itself put me to sleep.*

It is because of my automatic response to use that specific prayer last night that I believe something "not of this world" is occurring. I feel perhaps that my stepmother has commissioned one of the people that practice witchcraft to hinder our cause. Please, if you could write back to me with any form of advice I would truly appreciate it.

It is now late afternoon and I am afraid for the sun to set. Please respond.

TO OVERCOME FEAR, you must learn to reveal the simple, unwavering faith in God that is innate to your Divine soul, and experience closeness to our Creator through authentic Jewish meditation. God is called "the Eternity of Israel,"[1] and one who clings to Him clings to eternal life.

Before his passing, Rabbi Eliezer, the father of the Ba'al Shem Tov, told his five-year-old son, "Fear nothing but God."[2] Try to picture this scene in the inner eye of your heart. Throughout the day, try to remind yourself over and over again, until it becomes your second nature, that God is everywhere[3] and that He is with you always![4]

In general, vulnerability to negative forces can be avoided by feeling and behaving with humility and always expressing concern for and helping others, as the Talmudic axiom states, "Anyone who is compassionate towards people, God is compassionate towards him."[5] In the *Zohar*, the commandments are referred to as, "pieces of good advice."[6] If we selflessly follow God's "good advice" with compassion for others, without any desire to receive reward, God will bestow upon us manifest goodness.

Reciting the *Shema* with the intense concentration of your mind and heart is indeed a good thing. It is a *mitzvah* to recite the *Shema* twice daily, morning and night. Make a resolution to take this *mitzvah* upon yourself.[7] While reciting the *Shema*, strive to reach a similar level of intention to that which you reached after your nightmare and it will help you feel the

Divine presence with you throughout the day and serve as a reminder that ultimately there is nothing to fear in this world.[8]

Regarding dreams, as a rule, "dreams speak in vain."[11] The practical way to sweeten the negative impression that remains after a bad dream is by giving charity and doing good deeds.[12] Most importantly, remember to have faith and think positively. The famous Chassidic saying in Yiddish states, *tracht gut, vet zein gut,* "Think good and it will be good!" The Lubavitcher Rebbe explained that although a person may justify his fear by believing that his deeds are not meritorious enough to save him, nevertheless, he must put his faith in God who does good to those who deserve it and also

In the verse, "dreams speak in vain", the numerical value of the word וחלמת ("dreams") equals 484 which is the square of 22. This comes to teach us that dreams are essentially an irregular combination of the twenty-two letters of the Hebrew alphabet. We are taught in Chassidut that Joseph's ability to interpret dreams and reorder the chaotic meanderings of unrectified imagination stemmed from his profound knowledge of the Hebrew language which he achieved through successfully overcoming sexual enticement.[9]

The Hebrew word for "interpreter [of dreams]", is פותר, which is a permutation of the word תופר, "a tailor," who sews the pieces together in the right order. Another permutation of the same letters is פורת, which was the word used by Jacob to bless Joseph with fertility.[10]

The entire phrase, וחלמת השוא ידברו, equals 1,024 which is 32 squared, the number of letters in the entire Shema, indicating that Kriyat Shema is indeed the essential rectification for distressing dreams.

to those who do not deserve it, simply by merit of their perfect faith in Him.[13]

It is related in the Talmud[14] that King David had a bad dream every night. In Chassidut this is explained to mean that throughout the day, King David would constantly be clarifying the evil that met him and turning it into good. The bad dreams that he was shown at night were merely the completely evil residue that could not be clarified and turned into good. We are further taught that people often have bad dreams in order to nullify evil decrees.[15]

Witchcraft and the like have no influence or meaning; allow them no credibility.[16] Instead, fill your mind with positive, holy thoughts. In this way, there will be no room for troublesome thoughts to enter your head. Indeed, this is the best form of anxiety suppression.[17] This idea is expressed in the Torah's description of the pit into which Joseph was thrown, "And they took him and threw him into the pit; and the pit was empty, there was no water in it."[18] If the pit was empty, why does the Torah need to state that there was no water in it? Rashi replies to this question, "There was no water in it, but there were snakes and scorpions in it." In this analogy, Torah thoughts are likened to water, which, when absent, allows the presence of unwanted visitors in the form of snakes and scorpions, representing undesirable, troublesome thoughts, to enter the mind.

Hoping to hear good news from you soon!

With blessings of the Torah and the Land of Israel,

Notes:

1. I Samuel, 15:29. *Targum Yonatan* explains there that God is the "Master of the victories of Israel" (in Hebrew, *netzach* means both eternity and victory). The power to be victorious and overcome all evil forces that beset a person is purely from God.

2. A small child is naturally fearful of the world about him and when his father tells him that he should fear nothing except God Himself, he elevates the child's natural fear by connecting it to its root. This elevation of all fallen, childish fears releases a person's innate love of God. A Jew has an innate love of God the expression of which appears in the more concrete love for God's chosen nation of Israel and for the Land of Israel. However, in order to reveal that love, the person's fears must first reconnect to their root in the fear of God.

    Our daily prayers begin with the beautiful liturgical poem, *Adon Olam*, which inspires the rest of our prayers, according to the Chassidic dictum, "Everything goes according to the beginning." This prayer culminates with the verse:

    > In His hand shall I entrust my spirit,
    > When I am asleep and when I awake.
    > And with my soul, my body too,
    > GOD is with me, I shall not fear.

    Some people also have the custom of reciting this poem after reading the *Shema*, before going to sleep at night. In every situation we rely totally upon God, never fearing what the next moment may bring, for we are in His hands.

    Adon Olam (אדון עולם), means "Master of the Universe." The numerical value of these two words in Hebrew is 207, which is also the numerical value of אין סוף (meaning "Infinity," another appellation of God). In fact, אדון equals אין (61), and עולם equals סוף (146). God is in absolute control, He is the "Master." In Chassidut we are taught that one may even reach the highpoint in his prayer-arousal at this beginning point, therefore one should have great intent when reciting this prayer. The importance of this prayer is so great that one who has the correct intentions when reciting it is guaranteed that no prosecutor will interfere with his prayers and that his enemies will be repressed and even his evil inclination will be subdued (*Sefer Kitzur haShlah, Masechet Chulin, Inyanei Tefillah*).

3. Constant awareness of God's omnipresence, i.e., that "there is no place that is empty of Him" is the innate consciousness of Jewish wisdom (see *Sod Hashem Liyreiyav*, p. 169).

4. In Psalms (73:21-22) we find, "I am a boor, and I am ignorant, I am like an animal with You. Nevertheless, I am always with You, You hold onto my right hand." In these verses, King David, the author of Psalms, expresses his humility before God. Yet, immediately after these powerful expressions of his insignificance, and as a consequence of that awareness, King David reflects on the fact that he is always in God's presence and experiences His support. The more we sense our worthlessness before God, the more we feel His presence and His Providence and the closer we are to Him.

5. *Shabbat* 151b.

Walking in humility, or simplicity, is a manifestation of the *sefirah* of acknowledgment (הוד). In Hebrew, the letters of the word הוד permute to form the word דוה, meaning "anguish," suggesting that one who does not manifest this quality may become prone to anguish.

This also relates to the immune system of the body, which corresponds to the *sefirah* of acknowledgment. This system is the most susceptible to disorder and confusion, weakening its ability to distinguish between invading or diseased cells and positive, healthy cells.

As we rectify our ability to acknowledge and thank God for everything that we have and to relate to Him with wholehearted sincerity (the inner characteristic of the soul's rectified *sefirah* of acknowledgment), we are healed from illness and anguish (see *Body Mind and Soul*, p. 137).

In Kabbalistic permutation theory (see *Sod Hashem Liyreiav*, p. 102), the *sefirah* of acknowledgment, whose inner dimension is holistic simplicity (תמימות), reflects the *sefirah* of beauty, whose inner dimension is compassion (רחמים). Significantly, both the word תמימות and the word רחמים contain the letters that spell the word מים, meaning "water." This phenomenon finds expression in the verse, "As water [reflects] the face to the face, so does the heart of man to [another] man" (Proverbs 27:19). The Hebrew word for "face," used here, also means "inside," thus this verse can be read, "As [the word] "מים" reflects the inner dimension [of the *sefirah* of beauty] to the inner dimension [of the *sefirah* of acknowledgment], so does the heart of man to man."

The numerical value of the two remaining letters of רחמים is 208, or 8 times 26. The three remaining letters of תמימות equal 806, or 31 times 26. 26 is the numerical value of God's essential Name, *Havayah*. 8 times 26 plus 31 times 26 equals 39 times 26. 39 is equal to 26 plus a half of 26. Half of 26 is 13, the numerical value of אחד, meaning, "one." Thus these remaining five letters equal *Havayah* times *Havayah echad* (alluding to the first verse of the *Shema*, "Hear O Israel, GOD is our God, GOD is One").

6. *Zohar* II, 82b.

7. "And you shall review these things... as you lie down [to sleep at night] and as you rise [from sleep in the morning]" (Deuteronomy 6:7; 11:3).

8. "As a result of this [reviewing the words of the Torah in general and reading the *Shema* in particular] you will come to know God and to cling to His ways" (Rashi to Deuteronomy 6:7).

9. *Likutei Moharan* I, 19; see also *Transforming Darkness into Light*, p. 102.

10. Genesis, 49:22.

11. Zachariah, 10:2; the complete verse reads, "For the *teraphim* have spoken vanity, and the diviners have seen a lie, and dreams speak in vain, false is their comfort; therefore they go their way like sheep,

they are afflicted, because there is no shepherd." As we see from this verse, dreams appear in the same context as false prophets and other forms of witchcraft (see Letter 1).

12. In most Torah literature we find that fasting is recommended after experiencing a particularly troublesome dream. However, nowadays, since our bodies are physically weak and cannot endure extensive fasting, giving charity and doing good deeds is the recommended alternative.

13. *Likutei Sichot*, Volume 36, pp. 1-6.

The subject of positive thinking and overcoming fear is covered at length in our book, *Transforming Darkness into Light*, ch. 7.

14. *Berachot* 55b.

15. *Ma'amarei Admor Ha'Emtza'i, Hanachot* 5577, p. 247.

16. "All of these things are matters of deceit and falsehood... and it is not fitting for one of the nation of Israel... to be drawn after such nonsense, nor to attach any credence to them..." (Maimonides, *Mishneh Torah, Hilchot Avodah Zarah*, 11:17-18).

17. See *Transforming Darkness into Light*, ch. 4.

18. Genesis 37:24.

LETTER 8

BLESSINGS IN DISGUISE

I have a question regarding the removal of a curse on land and turning it into a blessing. Can you tell me any procedures or do's and don'ts concerning this? Any information will be appreciated.

IN THE *TANYA*[1] WE LEARN that any curse or apparent evil that befalls us in life is simply a blessing of such a high order that the goodness it contains cannot be integrated into the context of the limited spiritual level of our fallen world and the constrictions of our normative consciousness. Only in the future, or at present in moments of inspired spirituality, can the true goodness inherent in a curse be appreciated.[2]

Nonetheless, by contemplating the deeper implications of the two Hebrew words for "blessing," and "curse," we can begin to understand the practical manner by which to channel that goodness into our present lives.

The numerical value of "curse" (קללה) is 165, while that of "blessing" (ברכה) is 227. To reach 227 from 165, one must add 62. Thus, 62 is the number that transforms a curse into a blessing. The number 62 combines with the hidden positive potential latent in the curse itself and thereby reveals it to be a blessing.

There are two related expressions in Hebrew (comprising the same letters and the same common word, "good") each of which has a numerical value of 62: "very good" (טוב מאד) and "a good person" (אדם טוב).[3]

The phrase "very good" appears at the end of the Torah's opening account of creation: "And God saw all that He had created, and behold it was very good."[4] This phrase appears after the creation of man and refers to the rectified state of reality before the fall that resulted from the primordial sin of Adam and Eve in the Garden of Eden.[5] As a result of the sin, the earth was cursed together with man,[6] as we find in the verse, "And to Adam He said, since you listened to the voice of your wife and you ate from the tree from which I told you not to eat, cursed is the land for you..."[7] Although Adam was remiss in telling Eve to refrain only from eating of the fruit of the tree, the earth should originally have made the taste of the bark of the tree as the taste of its fruit, but it did not do so.[8] So the earth was cursed because, in part, it too was to blame for Adam's sin. Had the earth carried out its commandment as God commanded, there would have been no significance to Adam's laxity.[9]

The earth was further cursed after the second great sin of mankind, the murder of Abel by his brother Cain.[10] And so, in order to remove a curse on land and turn it into a blessing, one must return to the two original curses of the earth and rectify the sins that caused them.

Thus, to be a good person means to rectify the primordial sins of Adam and Cain.[11] Everyone is entrusted with a Divine spark and is responsible for rectifying the portion of the world[12] that relates to his own individual spark.[13]

In practice, to be a good person means using your unique talents to be creative in this world, to help others and to recognize and help reveal the goodness and Godliness in everything around you.[14] As difficult as it may be, you must try to understand that, in truth, all that happens is for the best, even when you cannot perceive that goodness. It is due to the nature of the human psyche that our mortal minds can generally only perceive a certain type of immediate or expected physical pleasure. So, if something appears as evil in our physical world, it is merely a reflection of our limited understanding of God's wondrous ways.[15]

With blessings of the Torah and the Land of Israel,

Notes:

1. "Just as one recites a blessing for his good fortune so must he also recite a blessing for misfortune" (*Mishnah Berachot* 9:5). The Talmud explains (*Berachot* 60a) that we should accept misfortune with joy, just as we rejoice in visible and obvious good, for it too is for the good, except that it is not apparent and visible to our mortal eyes, for it stems from the hidden world, which is higher than the revealed world (*Tanya*, ch. 26).

   "The life-force of all things, even those that we perceive as evil, as found within its source, is truly good. In fact, it is such a lofty manner of good that it remains faithful to its source, and as such is not comprehensible to man as good. In this it differs from the other form of good that is able to descend to so low a level that even mortals can perceive its goodness.

Because it retains the initial status of its revelation, this higher form of goodness is clothed in this world in a garb of pain and evil, inasmuch as its goodness has yet to be revealed to man" (*Igeret Hakodesh* ch. 11).

2. *Keter Shem Tov* 87. God created the world in such a way that His essential Name (*Havayah*) is concealed within the laws of nature that He set. The Divinity inherent in nature is expressed by the Name *Elokim* [the numerical values of א־להים (*Elokim*) and הטבע ("nature") are both 86]. Although it seems that the two Names are separate, at certain times we are able to reach the level at which it is clearly apparent that, "*Havayah* is *Elokim!*" (*Likutei Torah Bamidbar*, 8:1). For more about the Names of God, see *What You Need to Know about Kabbalah*, ch. 9.

3. *Bereishit Rabah* 9:12.

4. Genesis 1:31. The number 62, the numerical value of the phrase טוב מאד, is equal to 2 times 31. It is therefore significant that this phrase appears in the 31st (and final) verse of the initial account of creation in the Torah.

31 is the numerical value of God's Name *Kel* (א־ל), which is the Name associated with the *sefirah* of loving-kindness (see *What You Need to Know about Kabbalah* p. 151), upon which the world was constructed (Psalms 89:3).

The numerical value of Abraham (אברהם), the archetypal soul identified with the *sefirah* of loving-kindness, is 248, which equals 8 times 31 or 4 times 62. He was the first to rectify Adam's sin through his attribute of loving-kindness. God blessed Abraham that he should, "be a blessing [to others]" (Genesis 12:2). The power of blessing is given to Abraham, meaning that it is he (and his descendants, the Jewish people) who possesses the power to transform a curse into a blessing through the power of loving-kindness.

The sum of the two words for "blessing" and "curse" (ברכה and קללה) is 392, which equals 2 times 14² (196). A square number indicates perfection and a double square indicates a perfect complement, meaning that the combination of their inherent powers produces perfect inter-inclusion.

The average value of the two words is 196; when 196 is subtracted from the numerical value of ברכה (227), the remainder is 31. Similarly, when the numerical value of קללה (165) is subtracted from 196, the remainder is also 31. 31 is therefore the "wing" of the union. This is true of every such union of two numbers, the sum of which is an even number, in which there are two "wings" that extend in either direction to "bind" the unification. [We can express this mathematically in the following manner: if a, b are integers such that $a < b$ and $a \perp b = 2c$, then $c - a = b - c$. The two wings of the sum of $a \perp b$ are both equal to $c - a$].

In this case, the number 31 becomes even more significant, for the same letters that spell the Name אל also means "to," the primary vector force. The Hebrew word מקום, meaning, "place," or "space," has a numerical value of 186, which equals 6 times 31, the linear vector force, or 3 times 62, which relates to the 3 spatial dimensions. Abraham's name, with a numerical value of 248 (8 times 31, as mentioned), reflects perfect symmetry in the three dimensions of space (six directions), together with the fourth dimension of time (two additional directions). This reflects Abraham's ability to travel freely in time from past to future and from future to past, as alluded to in the verse, "and Abram traveled back and forth [lit., "going and traveling] to the Negev" (Genesis 12:9) The forward direction of time travel is to bring the world to its ultimate destiny, while the backward direction relates to the ability of "return to God out of love," to return to the past and transform iniquity into merit (*Yoma*

86b), revealing to the eyes of all that what had appeared to be a curse was in fact great blessing in disguise.

Today, the ability to move forward and backward in the time dimension is attributed to elementary particles. Indeed, it is amazing that 248 (the numerical value of אברהם, as above) is exactly equal to the numerical value of חלקיק, the modern Hebrew word for "elementary particle," and that there exists a theory, as yet unproven, that there are exactly 248 elementary particles in nature!

5. Before their sin, Adam and Eve were conscious of the Divine aspect of the world, however they were not yet at a stage at which they could incorporate that level of Divinity into their service of God and thereby raise all of creation to higher levels of consciousness. Had they waited until the onset of the Shabbat before they ate the fruit of the Tree of Knowledge of Good and Evil, they would have been elevated to even greater heights of consciousness, and all of creation would been elevated together with them. However, by their untimely tasting of the forbidden fruit, they lost their connection with the Divine and their consciousness sank into the lower worlds. Human consciousness and all of reality will be rectified when mankind once again reaches a state of experiencing the Divine without losing its connection with the physical world. See also Letter 1, note 9, above.

6. Indeed, in Hebrew the feminine form of "man" (אדם) means "earth" or "land" (אדמה).

In Hebrew, there are many examples of pairs of words that complement one another as the masculine and feminine forms of a noun. For instance, אור (masculine form, meaning, "light") and אורה (feminine form, meaning, "radiance"); טוב (masculine form, meaning, "good") and טובה (feminine form, meaning, "goodness"). In Chassidut it is explained that in these cases, the masculine form relates to the essence, while the feminine form of the word expresses its physical manifestation (see Rabbi Dov Ber, the second Rebbe of Chabad, *Sha'arei Orah*, *Sha'ar Hapurim*, 97a, 29). Similarly, in our case, the word for "earth" or "land," אדמה, is actually the feminine form of אדם, "man." So, the earth represents the physical manifestation of man's powers.

Yet, the earth was created before Adam was created from it. This suggests that even though we see the earth as the physical manifestation of man's powers, man may also be viewed as the tool by which the earth can reveal its powers of growth to their fullest capacity.

In general, we are taught in Kabbalah and Chassidut that just as a cause precedes its effect temporally, so its origin is higher than that of its effect. In our context, this indicates that the feminine "earth" has a higher source than the masculine "man."

7. Genesis 3:17.

8. Compare Genesis 1:11 with Genesis 1:12; Rashi Genesis 1:11

9. *Or Hachayim*, Genesis 1:17.

10. "Now, you are cursed from the earth which opened its mouth to take your brother's blood from your hand. When you work the earth, it will no longer give its strength..." (Genesis 4:11-12). Rashi explains that the second verse refers to an additional curse on the land. Nachmanides' differs in his opinion, explaining that the curse refers to the effects of Cain's labor on the land, which causes the earth to be less fruitful. Rashi understands that not complying with man's efforts is equivalent to cursing the earth itself, for giving its strength is its intended function in creation. The first curse, the result of Adam's sin, was that the earth would need to be cultivated in order to become fruitful (like a female, who is unable to produce offspring without first being impregnated). The second curse made the earth unable to perform its function and purpose in creation altogether (like a female who has become barren).

11. Adam was created "In the image of God" (בצלם א־להים; Genesis 1:27). The numerical value of each of the Hebrew words, "image" (צלם) and, "Cain" (קין) is 160, indicating that Cain was a direct continuation of Adam and was charged with the responsibility to rectify Adam's

sin. This is further alluded to by the fact that 160 is the product of multiplying the three letters of Adam's name (אדם): א (1) times ד (4) times ם (40) = 160!

12. When discussing this subject, the Rebbe would specifically use the term, "his portion in the world" (חלקו בעולם).

13. See *Tanya*, ch. 37.

14. Rabbi Levi Yitzchak of Berditchev composed the following song, called *The Dudele* (from the Yiddish *Du*, meaning "You"—addressing God in the second person) expressing this idea (translated here from the original Yiddish).

> Master of the Universe!
> I want to play You a Dudele.
> Master of the Universe!
> I want to sing You a Dudele.
>
> Where can I find You,
> O' Master of the Universe?
> Above—You, below—You.
> To the east—You, to the west—You
> To the south—You, to the north—You.
> You! You! You!
>
> And when things go well, it is You
> And if not—also You.
> But if it's You—it's good!
> You! You! You!

15. *Tanya*, ch. 11.

KITCHEN FIRES

Over the past year we have had a series of three kitchen fires. I do not know if we should be looking for a message from God in these events or what that message would be.

OUR SAGES TEACH US that any form of suffering that we experience in life should inspire us to ponder upon our deeds, to see whether perhaps our suffering is a sign from God that we should mend our ways.[1]

In the case of repeated kitchen fires, since the kitchen is generally the domain of the woman at home, she should be the one to contemplate her deeds, particularly in those areas that are specifically feminine.

There are three basic commandments in the Torah that are entrusted to women. Indeed, each of these three commandments is a holy "fire."[2]

Lighting Shabbat candles: This commandment corresponds to the *sefirah* of loving-kindness, which expresses the soul's attribute of love.

Keeping kosher: This commandment corresponds to the *sefirah* of might, which expresses the soul's attribute of fear.

Keeping the laws of family purity: This commandment corresponds to the *sefirah* of beauty, which expresses the soul's attribute of compassion.

These three commandments also correspond to three vessels located in the sanctuary[3] of the Holy Temple.[4] The candelabra, positioned in the south, the direction of loving-kindness, corresponds to lighting Shabbat candles; the table, positioned in the north, the direction of might, corresponds to keeping kosher; the incense altar corresponds to family purity.[5]

One of the reasons for lighting Shabbat candles is in order to intensify the harmony and peace that exist between husband and wife.[6] Since fire in general is a symbol of strife, we rectify it before Shabbat with a holy fire by lighting Shabbat candles in an atmosphere of great love between husband and wife and toward the entire family.[7]

We are taught in Kabbalah that fire emanates from the *sefirah* of might, which corresponds here to the commandment of keeping kosher. Since this is the commandment that most directly pertains to the kitchen, and fire is the medium used for cooking, it would seem that this should be the first place for the woman in this case to examine her deeds.

Eating is one of the activities that is shared between humans and animals. Nonetheless, if we eat with the correct intentions, we can elevate this activity to one of sanctity. For a

Jew, this means eating only kosher food and always expressing his gratitude to God by making the appropriate blessings before and after eating.[8]

If you are currently not keeping kosher, try to incorporate these laws into your home and to learn about their inner significance. If you are already keeping kosher, try to be more careful with doing so.[9]

Water is the medium that extinguishes fire. The laws of family purity culminate each month with the woman's immersion in the purifying waters of the *mikveh*, after which husband and wife may once more be physically intimate. The waters of the *mikveh* are the most potent means of overcoming marital strife,[13] the undesirable fire in the home, and of acquiring a holy fire of love and compassion[14] for one's spouse.

Love, in Kabbalah, represented in this case by the lighting of Shabbat candles, is the addition of a positive, attractive fire, while compassion, represented by the observance of the laws of

In Hebrew, the words for "man" (אִישׁ), and "woman" (אִשָּׁה), each contain the two letters of the word "fire" (אֵשׁ). The remaining letter yud (י) from the word "man" and the letter hei (ה) from the word "woman" combine to form one of God's Names, indicating that if the fire of the couple is aroused in holiness and is not merely the passion of physical desire, then God, as it were, becomes a partner in the union.[10] In addition, the letters of the word "fire" are the initial letters of one of the combinations of another of God's Names[11] and also the initial letters of "love" (אהבה) and "peace" (שלום) the two most important qualities that should prevail between husband and wife.[12]

family purity, is derived from the union of loving-kindness and might. Indeed, the *sefirah* of beauty is generally a uniting force that is capable of generating new life.

In general, if, after a person has contemplated his deeds and rectified them as necessary, he still experiences suffering of any form, he should know that his suffering is "a trial of love," i.e., an expression of the Almighty's great love for him, the purpose of which is to purify his soul and body in order to bring him closer to God in this world and bestow upon him infinite good in the World to Come.[15]

To conclude, there is a Yiddish saying quoted and explained in Chassidut, that states that a fire portends wealth: *Noch a sreifah vert men reich*! Since the first three attributes of the heart (mentioned above) are ordered: loving-kindness, might and beauty and since fire is principally a manifestation of might, the next attribute that should follow is the attribute of beauty, the inner experience of which is compassion.[16] How much the more so after three fires![17]

With blessings of the Torah and the Land of Israel,

Notes:

1. The Talmud (*Berachot* 5a) actually mentions three stages of contemplation through which a person should progress upon experiencing suffering, which correspond to the three stages of rectification that the Ba'al Shem Tov outlines in his teachings: submission, separation, and sweetening. The first stage, corresponding to the stage of submission, entails the person examining the quality of his deeds to see whether he perhaps did something wrong, and he should regret his actions and subsequently mend them.

If he finds no improper actions that could be the origin of his suffering, the second stage dictates that he should immerse himself in continual study of Torah. This is an act of separation, as Torah study separates a person from the vanities of this world.

If the person finds that a lack of Torah study is also not the apparent reason for his suffering, this is a sign that God, in His great love for him, is causing him pain in this world in order to allow him greater heights of spiritual reward in the World to Come (Rashi). Under such circumstances, the person should realize that these are pains of love and he should reflect God's love for him with his own love for God. This third stage is the ultimate sweetening of all suffering.

In the *Tanya* (*Igeret Hakodesh*, ch. 11), it is stated explicitly that life in this world is a test to assess whether we are drawn to the base desires of the flesh for our own egoistic gratification or whether our ultimate desire is to live a life that emanates from true Divinity. This echoes the conclusion the sages reach elsewhere in the Talmud (*Eruvin*, 13b) that it would generally have been better for man not to have been created at all, implying that in a certain sense all of our life in this world is suffering for the soul. However, the Talmud concludes, since we have been created, it is incumbent upon us to examine our deeds in order to remove those that are undesirable (corresponding to the stage of submission mentioned above) and to examine the quality of even the good deeds that we do in order to ascertain that they do not stem from undesirable intentions (corresponding to the stage of separation mentioned above. (See Rabbi Moshe Chayim Luzzato, *Mesilat Yesharim*, ch. 3).

If a person is a *tzadik*, a completely righteous person, then it is good that he was created, both for him and for his entire generation (see *Tosafot* to *Eruvin*, 13b). In the case of a *tzadik*, the descent of his soul into the physical world is considered "descent for the sake of ascent." It only remains to be said that the entire Jewish people are considered to have the potential to become *tzadikim* (Isaiah 60:21).

2. According to the sages (*Kidushin*, 56b), the very word קדש, "holy," is short for יקוד אש, meaning "burning fire," implying that all three fires are holy.

3. The *kodesh* (קדש), the holy area, which only *kohanim* (priests) were allowed to enter.

4. The Lubavitcher Rebbe established ten special campaigns to increase the observance of these three commandments together with another seven: *tefilin, mezuzah,* Torah, *tzedakah,* a house full of holy books, loving your fellow Jew and unity of the Jewish people, and Jewish education. Together, these ten campaigns correspond to the ten *sefirot* (from wisdom to kingdom; the superconscious crown, corresponds to God's campaign—to bring the Mashiach) as follows (explained at length in *Shechinah Beineihem*, ch. 6, note 7):

crown
Mashiach

understanding		wisdom
tefilin		**Torah**

knowledge
love and unity

might		loving-kindness
keeping kosher		**Shabbat candles**

beauty
family purity

acknowledgment		eternity
a house full of books		**Jewish education**

foundation
***tzedakah* (charity)**

kingdom
mezuzah

5. The word for "incense," (קטרת) is related to the word קישור, meaning "connection," relating in particular to the bonding of husband and wife (see *Devar Malchut, Tetzaveh* II, p. 351; *Shechinah Beineihem,* ch. 6, note 7).

6. See *Shabbat* 23b. In addition to the intention of **harmony**, there are two other intentions in lighting candles before Shabbat. The first is for **pleasure** (*Mishneh Torah, Hilchot Shabbat* 5:1) and the second is out of **respect** for the holiness of the day (*ibid.,* 30:5).

These three intentions correspond to the three heads of the three super-conscious levels of the soul:

- **marital harmony** corresponds to the Unknowable Head (*Radla*), the inner sense of which is faith, the basis of loyalty;

- **pleasure** is the inner sense of the Head of Nothingness (*Reisha De'ayin*);

- **respect**, demonstrates one's will and desire towards the Shabbat, corresponds to will, the inner sense of the Extended Head (*Reisha De'arich*).

In Kabbalah (*Sha'ar Hakavanot, Drushei Kabbalat Shabbat* 1), there are three unifications to intend on the word "candle," that combine to equal 250, the numerical value of the Hebrew word, נר: *Havayah* (26) *Ekyeh* (21); *Havayah* (26) *Elokim* (86) and *Havayah* (26) *Adni* (65). (These three unifications of God's Names also correspond to the three intentions mentioned above: marital harmony, pleasure and respect.)

7. This includes the extended family of the entire Jewish nation.

In general, we should have in mind that every *mitzvah* we perform is on behalf of the entire Jewish nation. Similarly, the Arizal taught that before the morning prayers we should accept upon ourselves the commandment to love our fellow as ourselves, so that our prayers emanate from that place in our souls at which all Jewish souls are one (*Pri Etz Chayim, Sha'ar Olam Ha'asiyah,* ch. 1; see also, *Derech Mitzvotecha, Mitzvat Ahavat Yisrael*). In lighting the Shabbat candles, the woman of the house lights the candles on behalf of all her family in love for all.

8. Non-Jews can also elevate their manner of eating to a more spiritual level by appropriately expressing their gratitude to God for the food that they eat. See *Kabbalah and Meditation for the Nations*, pp. 151-152.

9. Always being updated as to which foods are strictly kosher and overseeing all that takes place in the kitchen, ensuring that it be 100% kosher, is the greatest sign of a woman's fear of heaven and of her deepest concern for her family's spiritual and physical health.

   It is also important to regularly review the dietary laws of *kashrut* and to update one's knowledge of current *hechsherim* (kosher certification). For this and for questions that may arise concerning family purity, it is imperative to be in close contact with a qualified orthodox rabbi. Choosing a rabbi and a definite tradition (*minhag*) to follow throughout marriage is one of the things that a couple should decide upon even before marriage (as well as issues regarding the education and raising of the children that will, God willing, result from the union).

10. *Reishit Chochmah, Sha'ar Hakedushah* ch. 16; it is the custom to study this chapter before marriage.

11. א־ל ש־די; see at length in *Shechinah Beineihem* ch. 1.

12. *Ibid.*, p. 46.

13. The numerical value of the Hebrew word מקוה (*mikveh*), is 151, which is one more than the numerical value of the word כעס, meaning "anger" (150). This suggests that the purifying waters of the *mikveh* have the power to override all anger and strife between the couple.

   Similarly, the Arizal taught that to rectify anger one should fast 151 fasts (see *Tanya, Igeret Hateshuvah* ch. 2). Today, based upon the teachings of Chassidut (see *Igeret Hateshuvah* at length), we may accomplish this by donating $151 (or any other currency) to charity every time we get angry.

In addition, the Ba'al Shem Tov told his disciple, Rebbe Ya'akov Yosef of Polnoa (author of the book *Toldot Ya'akov Yosef*), that on a day that he becomes angry at his wife he should not compose Torah innovations, for, on such a day, his holy soul leaves him.

14. Compassion has the power to annul hatred and to arouse love in the heart. This is the secret of the phrase (Isaiah 29:22) "Jacob [personifying compassion] who redeemed Abraham [personifying love]" (*Tanya*, ch. 32).

15. *Berachot* 5a.

16. See, *Derech Mitzvotecha*, addendums, p. 198a.

17. The numerical value of the Hebrew word אש, "fire," is 301. Three fires therefore equal 3 times 301 = 903. 903 is the triangle of 42 (i.e. the sum of all integers from 1 to 42). In Kabbalah, 42 is the Name of God associated with creation, called, "the Name of 42 letters". This implies that just as in the covenant of marriage there are three partners in order to create new life—a body, formed by the two parents, is infused by God, the third partner, with a soul. Similarly, in the creation of the world there are three holy fires at play—the male fire, the female fire, and the fire that unites them. This is further indicated by the fact that the first word of creation, בראשית, "in the beginning," can be permuted into the two words ברית אש, meaning "a covenant of fire" (*Tikunei Zohar*, 12).

Since the word אש, "fire," has two letters, it thus possesses two permutations, the "forward" permutation (אש) and the "backward" permutation (שא). Thus, each of the three fires can be further subdivided into two. Accordingly, the sages speak of six fires (*Yoma* 21b). These six fires correspond to the four letters of God's essential Name, *Havayah*, from the final *hei* up to the *yud*, together with the two highest levels, which correspond to two levels within the tip of the *yud* as in the table below (see at length in *Sod Hashem Liyreiav*, pp.245-250):

letter of Havayah	type of fire	example
tip of *yud*	fire that consumes fire	the fire of the Divine Presence
	fire that repels fire	the fire of Gabriel
Yud	fire that consumes liquids as it consumes dry produce	the fire of the altar
hei	fire that eats and drinks	the fire of Elijah
vav	fire that drinks but does not eat	profane fire (a fever)
hei	fire that eats but does not drink	physical fire

LETTER 10

TWO BIRDS

In the last two months, I have had some interesting experiences and I am wondering what their significance is, if there is any.

On one occasion, as I was driving, a dove flew in front of the car. I could not avoid it. My car struck the bird killing it instantly. Then, just today on my way to the bakery, a sparrow flew up and again, my car struck the bird.

I am not sure if this is a coincidence or something else. Please let me know.

ALL THAT HAPPENS TO US, even the minutest, seemingly insignificant occurrence in life, is by Divine Providence; there are no coincidences and no accidents.[1]

Sometimes we are able to understand the significance of such events, gaining spiritual enlightenment and instruction from them, but generally, this is beyond our capabilities. When unable to interpret an event, we must humbly turn to God and say to Him in our hearts: You are surely trying to communicate with me, but, at present, I am unable to decipher Your language.[2]

The following story illustrates this idea:

A Spanish nobleman, who kept his Torah observance a secret, was caught in the act of keeping a *mitzvah* and condemned to be burned at the stake. However, he escaped the ordeal when an earthquake hit the city at the most profitable moment for him.

After this incident, the nobleman pondered over the miracle that had happened to him, unable to establish whether God had seen what would happen to him from the first moments of creation and had planned the earthquake for that very moment, so that he could escape, or whether the earthquake had been a natural occurrence and the miracle was that his execution had been arranged for the moment of the earthquake.

After receiving a number of unsatisfactory replies from various rabbis, the Spanish nobleman visited Mezhibuzh, the home-town of the Ba'al Shem Tov, and went to ask him his question.

The Ba'al Shem Tov invited the nobleman to accompany him to prayers in the synagogue, and on their way they saw a villager pulling a cartload of straw. A while later, they saw another man groaning in pain with toothache. He pushed his hand into the pile of straw and pulled out a single stalk, prodding it into his mouth, and the pain subsided.

The Ba'al Shem Tov then turned to the nobleman and explained that the stem that the man had pulled out was a special grass that eased toothache. He further explained that when God created the world, He had seen that this man would have toothache on this day and had designed things in such a way that the remedy would be available in the cart.

The goal is to live our lives according to the Torah, whose "path are paths of pleasantness and all its courses are peaceful."[3] God knows our limitations, and in such cases wants us to accept our experiences with the wholehearted faith that all that He does is for the best, without pondering too deeply over every event.[4] To assume that we can decipher God's meanings and intentions in every event that occurs is to assume that we can comprehend the incomprehensible and is truly a sign of exaggerated egocentricity.[5] So, while we must strive to understand and find meaning in what happens in our lives, we need to be careful not to overanalyze its significance. We must also recognize and accept that events sometimes occur for the purpose of teaching us to humbly accept certain situations in life with equanimity.

In Kabbalah, the spiritual dynamic needed to obtain the proper balance between understanding God's daily lessons to us and wholeheartedly following His directives, is encapsulated in the maxim "[The *sefirah* of] Understanding extends to [the *sefirah* of] acknowledgment [the attribute of wholeheartedness and sincerity]."[6] The inner experience of understanding is the joy[7] that comes with comprehension and intellectual achievement; nonetheless, understanding the limits of our comprehension and and acknowledging that we are unable to understand the significance of everything that befalls us in life,[8] is also a source of infinite joy and happiness.

We can now turn, in short, to your specific experience. In Kabbalah, a bird[9] represents the feelings of a soul.[10] To hit a bird can thus be understood to allude to hurting the feelings of another. The fact that you hit the birds unintentionally, by means of your vehicle, which is external to yourself, suggests that you may have unintentionally hurt someone's feelings by means of something external to yourself, while driving towards a destination. Try to remember if this may indeed have happened, and if so, ask forgiveness from the person whose feelings were hurt. In any event, be careful in the future to be sensitive to the feelings of others.

Also, in Hebrew, the root meaning, "acknowledgment" (הוד), also means "thanksgiving". So, try to be thankful for the Divine Providence that helped you to learn this lesson even if you do not fully understand it.

Gratitude is such an important concept in Judaism that the first words on a Jew's lips upon awakening in the morning are, "I thank You" (מודה אני). In fact, the very word for Jew in Hebrew (יהודי) stems from the root that means "to give thanks."

With blessings of the Torah and the Land of Israel,

There was once a king who wished to discover who in his kingdom had less troubles and worries than he himself had, for he was a king [and as such had few things about which to worry]. At night, he would go out and stand behind the houses to listen to what people were saying and hear all of their worries.

Once, he came across a tumbledown shack and saw a man playing a most cheerful tune on the fiddle, with a bowl of wine and a variety of foods set before him, and the man was very happy, full of joy, without t1he slightest worry. The king entered the shack incognito and asked the man how he fared and the man replied and offered the king food and drink, which he accepted. Later, the king lay down to sleep, and he saw how the man was full of joy, with absolutely no worries whatsoever. In the morning, upon awakening, the man accompanied the king on his way. The king then asked him, "Where do you get all this from?" The man replied, "My job is to fix anything that is broken. I go out in the morning to fix things for people, and once I have accumulated five or six gold coins, I buy myself food and drink."

Upon hearing this, the king thought to himself, "I will ruin this for him!" The king then went and announced that from now on, everybody should either fix their broken items themselves, or buy a new item.

The next morning when the man went out to look for work, nobody would give him anything to fix. Instead, he found himself work as a woodcutter until he had once again accumulated six gold coins. He bought himself a whole feast and was as joyful as ever, until the king once again visited him.

This scenario repeated itself a number of times, with the king preventing the man from continuing whatever work he had been doing until then.

Finally, discovering that even the most menial tasks that he had been doing had been disallowed by the king, the man recruited himself for day labor in the army. However the following day, the king decreed that no day laborers should be paid for their work that day. The man then took the sword that he had been given as part of his army uniform and temporarily pawned the blade, fixing a piece of wood in its place. That night, when the king came and saw the man eating and drinking and as joyful as ever, the king asked him how he had succeeded in finding the money for all of this and the man, in all simplicity, told his visitor of his actions.

The next day, the king told the commanding officer to bring the man to him. He then commanded him to behead someone who had been sentenced to death, quite aware of the fact that the man's sword blade was made of wood.

The man pleaded with the king, saying that he had never shed blood and that he should ask someone else to do the gory task, however, the king stood firm. The man asked if it was quite clear that the accused indeed deserved the death penalty, because as someone who had never shed blood before, he certainly did not wish to shed the blood of an innocent person. The king replied that the death sentence was quite clear.

Seeing that his pleas to the king fell on deaf ears, the man turned to God and beseeched aloud, "I have never shed blood in my life and if this man is not deserving of the death penalty, then the steel of the blade should turn into wood!" He immediately drew his sword and everyone present saw that it was made of wood. The king saw that he was such a good man, and he left him in peace.

Despite the difficulties that the man in the story had to suffer each day anew in order to earn his living, he still remained loyal to the king's commands, and at the end of each day he was joyful for what he had achieved, without any worries or complaints. His simple, wholehearted and joyful perspective on life was his greatest assest, even in times of great stress.[11]

Notes:

1. "Everything is in the hands of Heaven, except the fear of Heaven" (*Berachot* 33b; *Megilah* 25a). Nonetheless, should He choose to do so, God is capable of enlightening the world in such a way that even the fear of Heaven is in His hands, as in the verse "and a great fear fell upon them" (Daniel 10:7; see Rabbi Schneur Zalman of Liadi's *Likutei Torah, Bamidbar*, 15a). This means that not only are the events that happen to us in life by Divine Providence, even our spontaneous psychological reactions to these events are by Divine Providence. Our God-given gift of conscious choice is reflected primarily in our ability to control our emotions and urges. By contemplating the situation at hand we must consciously choose the appropriate emotion or feeling and arouse it in our hearts.

According to the Ba'al Shem Tov, there are two complementary levels of Divine Providence. "Not only is each movement of every type of creature made by Divine Providence—that being the life-energy given to the creature—but also, every individual movement of the creature serves a role in the realization of the general goal of all of creation. By combining and uniting every individual action ... the higher intention of the whole secret of creation is completed" (*Hayom Yom*, 28th *Cheshvan*).

In general, reality is divided into three levels: revealed miracles, miracles that appear through nature and natural causation. Nature conceals God's essence, as is expressed in the numerical equivalence between the Hebrew word for, "nature" (הטבע), and God's Name *Elokim* (א־להים; see Letter 8, note 2).

At the other extreme, revealed miracles thunderingly announce God's existence in an undeniable fashion, blatantly overriding the natural order of the world. Consequently, despite the enormous benefit that we gain from them, revealed miracles are not the way that God has chosen to illuminate the world on a daily basis.

Miracles that appear through nature are the way in which God speaks via the world. This is the knowledge that Abraham began to sow in the world when he took to pronouncing that God is *Kel Olam* (Genesis 21:11). In Chassidut we are taught that the innovation in using this specific Name, literally meaning "God-World", is that it indicates that in essence God and His world are one and the same.

2. Divine communication is received in each of the four spiritual Worlds in a different manner. It is only in the highest of the four Worlds, the World of Emanation, that a prophet becomes able to receive and comprehend explicit Divine speech. In the Worlds below Emanation, communication is received from Above in the form of parables and riddles. In the World of Action, in which our consciousness is generally present, we are only able to receive glimpses of Divine communication through hints and allusions that are generally incomprehensible to the average person.

The Hebrew word for "hint" or "allusion" (רמז) has a numerical value of 247. This is also the numerical value of the word meaning "luminary" (מאור), which in Kabbalah refers to a nuance of the essence of God's infinite light. This teaches us that in the manifestation of Divine Providence in the World of Action, the Divine essence is present and revealed to those who have eyes to see.

3. Proverbs 3:17.

4. For more on walking simply with God, see Letter 1.

5. In extreme cases, such egocentricity may result in false illusions such that may indicate psychic disorder. For instance, such a person may begin to believe that the radio is "speaking" (solely) to him etc. (see also Letter 1, note 13).

6. *Tikunei Zohar, tikun* 1 (7*a*); *Etz Chayim,* 35d and more. See also Letter 1, note 18(a).

7. There are five general levels of joy, each of which corresponds to a different level of the soul. The highest level of joy is the joy of the festival of Purim, during which we reach the apex of joy in the simple fact of our being Jewish (*Sod Hashem Liyereiav*, p. 259; see also *Likutei Moharan* II, 10).

    For more about joy as the inner experience of the *sefirah* of understanding, referring in particular to the joys of motherhood, see *What You Need to Know about Kabbalah,* pp. 105-6.

8. The *sefirah* of understanding belongs to the category of "the hidden things are to GOD our God" (Deuteronomy 29:28), whereas the *sefirah* of acknowledgment belongs to the category of "the revealed things are to us and to our children." From this it is clear that for most of us (those who have not yet reached the level of "the hidden things are to GOD our God"), understanding all that happens to us in life is beyond us. Even so, someone who walks simply and joyfully in the way of God, not pondering over the specific events that he encounters in his daily routine (realizing that he is unable to comprehend them), will nonetheless intuit the Divine messages that are being addressed to him.

The unification of the two powers of humility before God (the inner power of the *sefirah* of kingdom) and submission (achieved through sincere thanksgiving to God, the inner power of the *sefirah* of acknowledgment) create the purity of heart necessary to become a vessel receptive to intuitive inspiration and direction from God.

9. The numerical value of the Hebrew word for "bird" (צפור), is equal to the numerical value of the word "peace" (שלום). Birds are the harbingers of peace on earth. The Mashiach, "the Prince of Peace" (Isaiah 9:5), is the ultimate human herald of peace. The chamber of the Mashiach, his abode until such time as he is revealed, is called "the bird's nest" (קן צפור). The numerical value of קן צפור (526) is equal to the numerical value of "peace" when the name of each of its letters is written in full: שין למד וו מם.

We are taught in many places that the Mashiach will appear in two phases, *Mashiach ben Yosef* (Mashiach the son of Joseph) and *Mashiach ben David* (Mashiach the son of David). The numerical value of *Yosef* (Joseph) is 156, which is equivalent to the numerical value of a synonym for "bird" in Hebrew (עוף). Thus a bird, in Kabbalah, often represents *Mashiach ben Yosef*, who corresponds to the *sefirah* of foundation. Unless saved miraculously from death by the prayers of *Mashiach ben David* and of the Jewish people, *Mashiach ben Yosef* will be killed (see Rabbi Isaac Luria, *Sha'ar Hakavanot*, *Drushei Amidah*, 6).

10. See *Bava Kama* 90b. The expression in Hebrew is "the bird of the soul" (צפור הנפש). This idiom refers to that which most touches the heart, to the very core of the soul.

11. Rebbe Nachman of Breslov, *Sippurei Ma'asiot Mishanim Kadmoniot*, *Ma'aseh Bevitachon*. See also Rebbe Nachman's story of the *Chacham* and the *Tam* (The Wise Man and the Simpleton). The simpleton, representing the ideal of walking in holistic simplicity with God, was always happy. *Tam* (תם) is the root of the word *temimut* (תמימות), which is the inner attribute of the *sefirah* of acknowledgment (see Letter 1).

LETTER 11

THE CROW AND THE CAT

I had a dream about a crow following me and wanting to attack me. It was very scary at the time. A couple of nights later I had a dream of a cat coming after me. I was very scared that time as well. The very next night, I had a dream in which I was telling my dreams to a psychologist. When I told him about my dreams, he asked me what kind of bird I had seen in my dream the first night and I told him that it was a crow. Then I woke up! Can you help me understand the meaning of these dreams?

FIRST OF ALL, it is important to remember the words of the prophet: "Dreams speak in vain."[1] The sages teach us that the majority of dreams are nothing more than the extension of the thoughts that pass through our minds during waking hours.[2] Furthermore, when a person feels distress due to a dream, this is actually atonement for his or her misdeeds![3] The sages teach us that King David had a bad dream every night.[4]

With this in mind, it is possible to reflect on the symbols in a dream. From this reflection one may gain insight into one's connection and relationship to his Creator.

From a general perspective, your dreams seem to allude to a fear of being chased, with a will to solve the problem (the last dream). The true solution is strengthening your belief and faith in God, who protects you, while simultaneously living a Jewish life based on Torah directives. This is the true power of protection that guards us from both physical and spiritual adversaries.

Crows are infamously renowned as cruel predators and even as parents who neglect their young. Even so, it was the crows who God chose as His emissaries to feed the Prophet Elijah when he fled to the Karit River at God's command, at the onset of the drought that Elijah himself had decreed upon the land.[5] From this we learn that it is incumbent upon us to break any natural, cruel crow-like tendency we may possess when we first come to do charitable deeds, to transform it into compassion and to adopt a charitable attitude towards our fellows.[6]

As a symbol, the crow exists both in holiness and in unholiness, since God has created everything in our world according to the principle of "this opposite this," meaning that every positive entity has a "flip side" that manifests negatively.[7]

The unholy crow refers to Orev (literally meaning, "crow") and Ze'ev, the two leaders of Midian, who were killed by Gideon.

King David was pursued by a diversity of enemies throughout his lifetime, however, through his faith in God (expressed in the psalms he wrote), his life was miraculously spared. This he acknowledges in the verse, "For my father and my mother have abandoned me, but GOD will gather me up."[8] In this quality, King David is similar to the crow's fledglings, who are abandoned by their parents and cry out to God to save them, as we find in the song of the crow in *Perek Shirah*,[9] "Who prepares the food for the crow as its children cry out to God."[10] King David himself is thus the crow of holiness.[11]

This is further alluded to in the verse he wrote: "Guarantee your servant's wellbeing, do not let the arrogant wrong me."[12] The word עֲרֹב, "guarantee," stems from the same root as the word עֹרֵב, "crow," but, as opposed to the cruel nature of the unholy crow, this verse alludes to the holy quality of the Jewish people as mutual guarantors who feel an innate responsibility for one another. This state of mutual responsibility (עַרְבוּת), took legal effect from the time that the Jewish People entered the Land of Israel,[13] which in Kabbalah represents the consciousness of the *sefirah* of kingdom, the spiritual level of King David who suffered most when forced to leave the Land of Israel.[14]

On a somewhat more mundane level, fear of being attacked by a crow is a "farmer" syndrome. To the farmer, the crow represents territorial invasion, trespass and a threat to his crops.

In order to prevent attack, the farmer takes steps to ward off predatory crows by extending his own presence in the field even when he is not physically present, by means of a scarecrow. Similarly, in order to overcome a fear of being attacked by various types of "crow," you have to learn how to intimidate the crow, rather than allowing the crow to intimidate you.

The song of the cat in *Perek Shirah*, is "I shall pursue my enemies and overtake them. I shall not return until I have annihilated them."[15] In this verse, its author, King David once again, expresses his conviction to pursue his enemies, the enemies of Israel and of God, and not to return until he has totally annihilated them.[16] Thus, King David is both the holy crow and the holy cat.

Fear of being chased by a cat suggests a "mouse" complex. The song of the mouse in *Perek Shirah* (which immediately follows the song of the cat, in response, as it were, to the cat),[17] expresses the corrected consciousness of the mouse, the confession of his past misdeeds, "And You are righteous in all that overcomes me, for you have done truth and I have done evil."[18] The mouse has a guilt complex for having stolen that which does not belong to it. The rectification of a fear of being chased by a cat is, therefore, to admit and rectify one's misdemeanors (something that should be done before being obliged to do so by being caught in the act.)[19]

More generally, overcoming fear of wild animals depends upon the rectification of sexual iniquities. The *Zohar* teaches us that wild animals can only harm someone who has sinned in this sphere, since such sins inhibit the appearance of the Divine image of man, making it unable for the animal to distinguish that this is a man and not a beast. In contrast, someone who is careful to guard himself from any degradation in this area retains his Divine image; the animal recognizes this and keeps its distance.[20] Indeed, the story is told of Rabbi Menachem Mendel of Vorki, that once when he was traveling on the road, wild animals attacked him. He said, "I do not fear them, for I have not blemished myself [with sins of the flesh]."

From our meditation so far upon the symbols you saw in your dreams, we see that in your first dream fear of the crow indicates a fear of being invaded and stolen from while in the second dream, fear of the cat indicates a sense of guilt[21] for having once stolen and now being pursued (perhaps by the police, the "cat"). Becoming aware of these two apparently contrasting complexes now makes it necessary to see a psychologist, as in your third dream.

The classic psychologist, the role model one should seek when

Guilt complexes and depression arise as the result of the inability of the ego to accept its innate lowliness, "How could it be that I [who am so 'important'] could fall to such actions?" This state of mind is the antithesis of the correct consciousness necessary to truly reconnect to the Creator.

Rectification of one's past should be approached wholeheartedly through a sense of true humility and joy, by realizing that, if we are able to distance ourselves from the Divine, how much the more so must we be capable of coming infinitely closer through returning to Him.

looking for a therapist or counselor, is someone who has the qualities of Joseph.[22] Joseph was the archetypal dream interpreter of the Torah who mastered the skill of reordering the chaotic meanderings of the unrectified imagination as they appear in dreams and rendering them into a clear image.[23]

In your third dream the psychologist asked which bird you saw because in general birds are associated in Kabbalah with the *sefirah* of foundation (the numerical values of Joseph and "bird" are both 156).[24] However, the crow (and the cat too), is associated with the *sefirah* of kingdom (David), as we have illustrated. Thus we have both Joseph (the psychologist and birds in general) together with David (both the crow and the cat). Together, these two are the typical messianic combination, and indeed this is beautifully alluded to in the numerical values of the two creatures, for the average value of "crow" (עֹרֵב; 272) and "cat" (חָתוּל; 444) is 358, the numerical value of *Mashiach* (מָשִׁיחַ)![25] The fact that the combined numerical value of cat and crow is equal to twice the value of *Mashiach* alludes to the ultimate union of Mashiach the son of Joseph and Mashiach the son of David within the one Mashiach.[26]

Symbols in dreams are often influenced by one's local culture as we are taught in the Talmud. The Talmud states that someone who sees a cat in his dream in a place where a cat is called *shunra* (in Aramaic), will be awarded a pleasant song, since *shunra* is an acronym for *shirah na'ah*, "pleasant song," whereas if his dream was in a place where a cat is called *shinra* (according to another Aramaic vernacular) then a bad change will befall him, since *shinra* is an acronym for *shinui ra*, "bad change."[27] Thus it is important to add that in American culture crows, especially scary crows, remind one (whether consciously or unconsciously) of scarecrows, as noted above. The scarecrow is generally constructed in the form of a cross,[28] the symbol of the religion that is diametrically opposed to Judaism (even though, as with everything else in God's world, it serves a Divinely ordained purpose on the way towards complete redemption).[29] The crow in this case represents Esau, who, in Kabbalah, is the spiritual origin of that religion, meaning that being attacked by a crow may allude to one being attacked or bothered by idolatrous thoughts deriving from the culture of that religion. In Chassidut we are taught that to rectify such thoughts, one should simply ignore them, while immersing oneself in Torah study, in particular the study of matters pertaining to the final redemption with the coming of the true Mashiach.

With blessings of the Torah and the Land of Israel,

Notes:

1. Zachariah 10:2.

2. *Berachot* 55b.

3. When accompanied by a genuine desire to improve one's behavior. (See *Shulchan Aruch, Orach Chaim* 220 and *Mishnah Berurah* 6).

4. *Berachot* 55b. This means that nightmares are a phenomenon that reflects the *sefirah* of kingdom, of which it is said (Proverbs 5:5), "Her legs descend unto death...." Awakening from such a dream is thus comparable to kingdom returning to its origin of Divine consciousness in the World of Emanation (where no separate state of

self-consciousness exists). We may learn from this that the absence of Divine consciousness is like living a nightmare.

5. I Kings, 17:6.

6. *Likutei Moharan* II 4:1.

7. The first appearance of the crow in the Torah is after the flood, when Noah releases it before sending the dove to test for dry land. The purpose of the crow's release from the ark is not explicit in the verses of the Torah. However, the sages teach us that Noah expelled the crow for having had relations with the female crow, against God's commandment that no creature cohabit during their sojourn in the ark. This in particular indicates the lustful nature of the crow, who is unable to restrict its natural instincts. This quality of the crow is similar to the wolf syndrome, in which the victim experiences a fear of personal invasion. For a more detailed discussion of these ideas see *Body, Mind, and Soul*, ch. 4.

The crow and the wolf are personified by the two enemies of Israel Orev ("crow") and Ze'ev ("wolf") against whom Gideon fought and was victorious.

This victory was predicted when Gideon overheard someone relating a dream to his friend. The friend interpreted this dream to mean that Gideon would be victorious (Judges 7:25; see also note 9 below). A dream that someone else dreams about a person is considered to be a meaningful dream, likely to come true (*Berachot* 55b; see also letter 12, note 1).

8. Psalms 27:10.

9. For a description of *Perek Shirah*, see Letter 1, note 10.

10. Job 38:41.

11. The sum of the numerical value of the letters of King David's name when spelled in Hebrew, with each letter doubled and then squared, equals the numerical value of "crow" (ערב). This is a calculative process referred to in Kabbalah as *kiflei kiflayim*, which is computed as follows: The numerical values of the three letters of David's name

(דוד) are 4, 6 and 4; (2 times 4)² plus (2 times 6)² plus (2 times 4)² = 272, which is the numerical value of "crow" (ערב), as mentioned. (See beginning of *Sefer Karnayim*, on the verse, *Arov avdechah letov* and the *Dan Yadin* commentary there.)

12. Psalms 119:122.

13. Upon entering the Land of Israel, the Jewish nation assembled on Mt. Gerizim and Mt. Ebal to hear the reading of the blessings and the curses, as God commanded them to do while still in the wilderness (Joshua 8:33; Deuteronomy 11:29). In response to each blessing and each curse the entire Jewish people replied "Amen!" This ceremony initiated the binding responsibility that the Jewish nation accepted upon themselves upon entering the Land of Israel (see Rabbi Yosef Dov Soloveitchik, *Kol Dodi Dofek*).

14. See I Samuel, 21:11-22:4.

15. Psalms 18:38.

16. King David is one of the four kings whose differing levels of faith in God when faced with an adversary, are noted by the sages (introduction to *Eichah Rabah*, ch. 30). These four are David, Asa, Jehoshaphat and Hezekiah. King David prayed to be actively involved in his wars and to be victorious, whereas the other kings each prayed to succeed in more passive victories, so much so that the last king, Hezekiah, said, "I do not have the power to kill, nor to chase after my enemies, nor to sing praises, rather I will sleep in bed, and You, God, will do everything." God agreed to do as each king requested. Each king was afraid that his sins would prevent him from succeeding by merit of his own deeds, and he therefore requested that God take a more active part in the war. King David was the only one who had the strength of faith to believe that through guarding his deeds and carefully assessing them, he would merit to be the direct instrument of God's salvation. King David's cleanliness of deed is similar to the cleanliness and modesty that distinguish the behavior of the cat from that of other animals (see

Eruvin, 100b). For a more detailed discussion of this idea, see our book in Hebrew *Lev Lada'at*, pp. 105-107.

17. This is according to the version of *Perek Shirah* cited in the book *Beit Elokim* by the *Mabit*.

18. See Nehemiah 9:33.

19. See at length (in Hebrew), *Malchut Yisrael* vol. 3, p. 217.

20. See *Tanya* ch. 24.

21. See *Lev Lada'at*, elucidations on *Perek Beavodat Hashem*.

From this idea we can see that these phobias (fear of invasion and guilt complexes), are both related to the four lower *sefirot*, which all relate to the wolf syndrome as explained in *Body, Mind, and Soul*, ch. 9.

22. See *Transforming Darkness into Light*, ch. 9.

23. In the Torah, Jacob blesses his son Joseph with fertility, using the phrase, *ben porat* (בן פורת). The letters of the word פורת can be rearranged to form the word תופר, "sew," or פותר, "dream interpreter," alluding to Joseph's ability to correctly "sew" and reorder the unordered letters that appear in dreams into words with sensible meanings. This he achieved in a similar manner to the High Priest who correctly interpreted the messages of the letters illuminated on his breastplate. This is related to Joseph's ability to guard and purify his sexual desires, the quality for which he is renowned as, "Joseph the Righteous."

24. See also, Letter 10, note 9.

25. The numerical values of "Mashiach" and "snake" (נחש) are both 358, indicating that just as both the animals which appear in your dream have a "flip-side," so too, the Mashiach has a negative manifestation.

The difference between the average value (358) and the value of each of the two words that it unites (272 and 444) is 86, which is also the value of God's Name *Elokim*, the manifestation of Divinity in nature. In Kabbalah, this difference is called the "wing" value. For a mathematical explanation of a "wing" number, see Letter 8, note 4.

26. See also Letter 10, note 9.

27. *Berachot* 56b. In the time of the Talmud, these were two Babylonian vernaculars. In more recent times, these two vernaculars are echoed in the way that Russian Jews and Polish Jews vocalize the word (implying that Russian cats are "pleasant songs," whereas Polish cats are "bad changes"). Indeed, these two forms complement one another, for when added together, *shunra* (557) and *shinra* (561) equal 1118, which is the numerical value of the essential expression of Jewish faith, the *Shema*: "Hear O Israel, GOD [*Havayah*] is our God [*Elokim*], GOD [*Havayah*] is one." The *Shema* proclaims the absolute unity of these two Names, *Havayah* (26; representing God's transcendence and supernatural providence) and *Elokim* (86; representing God's immanence and providence within the natural order). Indeed, 1118 is also the lowest common multiple of the values of these two Names. Thus the absolute unification of both aspects of God's manifestation is reflected, in our lower reality, in the unification of the *shunra* and the *shinra*, two vernaculars for one and the same cat.

We can further understand this idea when considering that although all that emanates from Above (referring to the Name *Havayah*) is only goodness (a "pleasant song"), when that goodness manifests through the natural causes of the world (via the Name *Elokim*, which has the same numerical value as the Hebrew word meaning "nature"), it is often perceived by us as a "bad change," a change for the worse, God forbid. However, in truth, these are actually one and the same, and "no evil descends from Above" (see letter 8).

28. In Hebrew, a cross is called שתי וָעֵרֶב which literally means "the warp and woof" threads of woven fabric. The word עֵרֶב is a variant reading of the same letters that form the word עָרֵב, "crow." Interestingly, even in English, the words "cross" and "crows" are phonetically similar.

29. "Nevertheless, the intent of the Creator of the world is not within the power of man to comprehend, for [to paraphrase Isaiah 55:8] His ways are not our ways, nor are His thoughts our thoughts.

[Ultimately,] all the deeds of Jesus of Nazareth and the Ishmaelite who arose after him [i.e., Mohammed] will only serve to pave the way for the coming of the Mashiach and for the improvement of the entire world, [motivating the nations] to serve God together, as it is written [Zephaniah 3:9], "For I shall then make the peoples pure of speech so that they will all call upon the Name of GOD and serve Him with one accord."

How will this come about? [As a result of these religions,] the entire world has already filled with talk of the Messiah, as well as of the Torah and the commandments. These matters have been spread among many [formerly] spiritually insensitive nations, who discuss these matters as well as the various commandments of the Torah. Some of them [i.e., the Christians] say: These commandments were true, but are not in force in the present age; they are not applicable for all time. Others [i.e., the Moslems] say: Implied in the commandments are hidden concepts that cannot be understood simply; the messiah has already come and revealed them.

[The stage is thus set so that] when the true Messianic king will arise and prove successful, his [position becoming] exalted and uplifted, they will all return and realize that their ancestors endowed them with a false heritage; their prophets and ancestors caused them to err. (Maimonides [uncensored edition], *Hilchot Melachim*, ch. 11; see also *Kabbalah and Meditation for the Nations*, pp. 165-170).

LETTER 12

AROUSAL FROM ABOVE

I have had several very significant dreams that have so disturbed me.

I spent much time with my Jewish grandmother on my father's side when I was younger (my mother is not Jewish). We were very close until the time she became very ill; she died a few years ago. I was loved but not really grounded in any particular truth. I have set foot in a synagogue once that I know of, and I have visited some festivities sponsored by a Jewish community center.

In the first dream, my grandmother took me to the Jewish community center. She showed me a rack of recital gowns for ballet and told me to choose one. So I did. I did not know that there was anyone in the center. I was on a platform, and I began worshipping God with my heart so intensely that I began to spin very gracefully, and I was lifted straight up into the air. I then descended. There were now some young Jewish girls standing there with my grandmother. At this point, my heart was flooded, and I felt as if I would burst. And I grabbed their arms and said, "I have found the

Messiah, and I am a completed Jew!" But they would not hear me.

My grandmother then took me and we went out to a narrow walkway towards another building, which I knew was a learning center. Without a word said, my grandmother's eyes and mine met, and we welled up in tears with the same thought of how sad it was. For I knew they had the most beautiful books, but the building in which they were was in need of repair. There was dampness as the building had been neglected, and I was afraid the mold would set in to those precious books. And the dream ended.

The next dream I was in a room and my grandmother was there again. There were three tapestries hanging on one of the walls. And there were two men who were with my grandmother. I knew they were "prophets of old" and even dressed so.

The last dream, again I was in a Jewish community center, attending a festival of some sort. And all over the white columns there was Hebrew lettering, but I couldn't see it until an invisible hand had taken ink and rolled it over the columns, then the Hebrew letters all came forward.

No one I know really seems to have any insight into what these dreams may mean. I would greatly appreciate any wisdom you might pass on to me.

WHEN WE AWAKEN from a meaningful dream, especially a dream that we have dreamt more than once (whether the dreams are exactly the same or similar to one another),[3] we must first take to heart that the ultimate purpose of our dreams is to arouse us to draw closer to our Creator through proper thought, speech and action, both in our inner lives and in the way we relate to those around us.[4] With this in mind, it is possible for us to reflect on the symbols we see in dreams and on the message that they convey.

Clearly, it is the soul of your Jewish grandmother who is the source of inspiration of your dreams.[5] Her soul is your gateway to Judaism.

Most significantly, the numerical value of the word meaning "grandmother" (סבתא), is identical to the numerical value of, "intuitive intelligence" (תבונה). Kabbalah teaches us that within the sefirah of understanding, there are two partzufim (personas), each of which represents a different faculty of intelligence, "intuitive intelligence" and "the supernal mother" (אמא עילאה). "The supernal mother" represents the power to grasp the insights that come from the sefirah of wisdom, so that they do not disappear back into the realm of the super-conscious. "Intuitive intelligence" represents the power to fully absorb and integrate one's intellectual understanding into one's psyche. This is a process of spiritual impregnation, which gives birth to the deepest emotions of the soul, the principal one of which is the love for God that is hidden deep in the heart, as expressed in the verse, "Deep waters [waters symbolize love] are the counsel of a man's heart, and a man of intuition can draw it out".[1] The power of intuitive intelligence is also the gateway to reconnecting with our Creator, as we find in the phrase, "and his heart shall understand and he shall return and be healed."[2]

In the first dream, after experiencing a spiritual elevation through worshiping God, you find yourself together with your grandmother, but now in the company of other Jewish girls. You are being drawn into the collective soul of the Jewish people. To become a "completed Jew" is in truth a messianic experience. The girls do not hear you, because before learning Torah, you are unable to address them in their language. The books in your dream represent the Torah and its commandments, the lost legacy of your father's family. The learning center has been neglected and is in need of repair. This hints at what may be your life's mission—to help repair the Torah's learning center.

In your next dream, the three tapestries allude to the three parts of the Bible: the Five Books of Moses, the Prophets, and the Writings. The two "prophets of old" whom you saw together with your grandmother, allude to the two greatest, archetypal prophets of Israel, the two brothers Moses and Aaron.[6] The presence of your grandmother together with these two prophets allude to their sister, Miriam.[7] In general, we are taught that it is the soul of Miriam that arouses Jews to reconnect with their Judaism and inspires non-Jews to convert.[8]

The meaning of your last dream is most profound. We are taught that the Creator, continuously creates reality by means of the letters of the Hebrew alphabet (in particular, by means of the permutations of the letters of the Ten Sayings of Creation that appear at the beginning of Genesis[9]). The letters are the Divine channels of consciousness, the life-force that permeates reality and the building blocks of creation.[10] But they are invisible to our physical eyes. The letters of creation become visible when the ink[11] of the letters of the Torah is rolled over them (from an unseen source, the Giver of the Torah). When we merit seeing reality through the prism of the ink of the letters of the Torah, we become able to perceive God's continual act of re-creation of the entire universe, down to its most minute detail, by means of the Hebrew letters.[12]

To conclude, the meaning of all of your dreams is that you are being inspired and encouraged from Above to draw near to the Jewish faith and to connect to and learn from the Torah, the blueprint of all creation.

Since your mother is not Jewish, according to Jewish law you are not considered a Jew.[13] However, as your father is Jewish (because his mother, your grandmother, was Jewish), Jewish law advises that you study as much as you can about Judaism, Torah, Chassidut and Jewish tradition, with the thought of proceeding towards undergoing a proper Orthodox conversion, thus truly becoming "a completed Jew."[14]

Wishing you all the best. Please feel free to write with any questions you may have.

With blessings of the Torah and the Land of Israel,

Notes:

1. Proverbs 20:5.

2. Isaiah 6:10.

3. There are certain types of dreams that the sages teach us are particularly meaningful (and most likely to come true). These are: a dream from which one awakens in the morning; a dream which one's

friend dreams about him; a dream whose solution appears together with the dream; and also a dream which is dreamt more than once (*Berachot*, 55b).

These four types of especially meaningful dreams correspond, in Kabbalah, to the four letters of God's essential Name, *Havayah*, as follows:

letter of *Havayah*	*sefirah*	type of dream
yud	wisdom	a dream from which one awakens in the morning
hei	understanding	a dream which one's friend dreams about him
vav	knowledge	a dream whose solution appears together with the dream
hei	kingdom	a dream which is dreamt more than once

Let us explain this correspondence in short:

- Awakening in the morning, together with the rising (the awakening) of the sun, is a new flash of insight, an experience of wisdom, corresponding to the *yud* of *Havayah*.

- The first *hei* of *Havayah* corresponds to the *sefirah* of understanding, which is referred to as the "companion" of wisdom (*Zohar* III, 4a). In Kabbalah we are taught that the *sefirah* of understanding is the place where souls are connected to one another. In our context, this represents a dream that one's friend dreams about him.

- The inner soul of the *vav* of *Havayah* is the *sefirah* of knowledge, which is referred to as "the key that contains six," i.e., the key that opens the six "chambers," or emotions, of the heart: loving-kindness, might, beauty, victory, acknowledgment and foundation (*Zohar* II, 177a). Knowledge fills the emotions with meaning, and so corresponds to a dream whose solution appears together with the dream.

- The last of the letters of *Havayah*, the final *hei*, corresponds to the *sefirah* of kingdom. Indeed, it was a king—Pharaoh—who was shown a dream twice, each time in a different setting, first with cows and then with ears of corn, both with the same message: seven years of plenty will be followed by seven years of famine (Genesis 41:1-8).

[Pharaoh's dreams were interpreted by Joseph, who himself had previously dreamt twice (in two different settings) that he was to rule over his brothers (Genesis 33:5-9). Hearing Pharaoh's repeated dream [repetition indicative of sovereignty (kingdom), as above] reinforced his conviction that his own dreams were true, and that indeed he was destined to rule (over Egypt, where his brothers would come to bow down to him). This inspired him to add to the interpretation of Pharaoh's dreams that it would be wise for Pharaoh to appoint a viceroy to rule over Egypt during the period of plenty and the period of famine that would follow, alluding, of course, to himself.]

A potential convert to Judaism also relates to the *sefirah* of kingdom, and to the World of Action, whose Divine life-force derives from the *sefirah* of kingdom. In order to arouse the potential convert to take action and make the existential leap of faith necessary to become a Torah abiding Jew, a servant of the One God of Israel, he is often reinforced from heaven by repeatedly being shown relevant dreams.

4. This is true whether we dream good dreams or bad dreams, dreams that seem to make sense or dreams that make no sense. Good dreams are to arouse us to serve God with joy; bad dreams, to arouse us to be in awe of God and to do *teshuvah*, i.e., return to God; dreams that make sense suggest that we should serve God within the limits of our own innate common sense while dreams that make no sense indicate a service of God that knows no rational bounds.

5. The sign of spiritual connection to other souls is love and an innate feeling of closeness.

6. Moses, who brought God's word to the people in the form of the Torah, is identified as, "the King's escort," who attends the King (the

"Groom") in His descent towards His people, while Aaron, who kindles the lamps of the candelabra in the Temple, is "the Queen's escort," who accompanies the Queen (the "Bride"), to join the King under the wedding canopy.

In the Torah we find that God explicitly states the difference between Moses' level of prophecy and that of Aaron or any other prophet, "If there should be a prophet of GOD, I make Myself known to him in a vision, in a dream shall I speak in him. Not so My servant Moses... mouth-to-mouth do I speak with him, in a clear vision and not with riddles, and he gazes at the image of GOD" (Numbers 12:6-8). The prophecies of Moses were the most direct prophecies received by any mortal.

The Hebrew words for "a clear vision" and "a mirror" are spelled with the same letters, only with a different vowel beneath the letter *alef* (both are written as "מראה"). The letter *alef* serves as a window to infinity, reflecting the paradox of Divinity in the physical world (see *The Hebrew Letters*, pp. 26-27). From here the sages teach us that Moses perceived his prophecy through "a transparent pane," while Aaron (and all other prophets) perceived his prophecy through "a translucent pane" (or "mirror image"). This is expressed in the opening word of their prophecies: the word which distinguishes Moses prophecies is "this" (זה): "**This** is the thing that God has commanded," while Aaron and all other prophets received their prophecies with the less exact introduction of "so" (כה): "**So** said God."

Aaron prophesized in Egypt, where even Moses began his prophecies with the word "so" (see for example Exodus 3:14-15). However, Aaron prophesized before Moses came to redeem the people, and his prophecies are not recorded explicitly in the Torah. The "so" cited for Aaron introduces the priestly blessing given to Aaron and his offspring (Numbers 6:23). All other prophets begin their prophecies with "so", albeit at a lower level than Aaron, whose level relates to that of his brother Moses, as discussed in Kabbalah regarding the inter-inclusion of "so" within "this." This inter-inclusion is indicated in the verse that refers to the two brothers,

Moses and Aaron, "How good and how pleasant it is that brothers dwell together" (Psalms 133:1).

The total numerical value of the four words, "clear vision" (מראה), "this" (זה), "mirror" (מראה) and "so" (כה) is 529, which is also the numerical value of the word meaning "pleasure" (תענוג). Pleasure is the middle head of the soul's super-conscious crown, known as "the head of nothingness," which is identified in Kabbalah as the origin of prophecy in the psyche.

Now, let us see something further about the relationship between pleasure and these two levels of prophecy. 529 is also the square of 23, while the sum of *zeh* and *koh* equals 37. 23 and 37 are the numerical values of the companion words *chayah* ("living one") and *yechidah* ("singular one"), which are the names of the highest two levels of the soul. These two numbers appear consecutively as the sixth and seventh integers of the following additive series (explained in greater depth in our forthcoming book on the principles of Torah mathematics and the "Golden Section"):

1 4 5 9 14 **23 37** 60 97 157 254 …

As noted, the words "clear vision" and "mirror" have an identical numerical value of 246 which is also the numerical value of the phrase meaning, "the image of God" (צלם א-להים). Man was created in "the image of God," and, when he manifests the essence of his Divine soul, he becomes worthy of conveying God's word in prophecy to mankind.

The first word of the phrase, צלם, meaning "image," is constructed of three letters: *tzadik-lamed-mem*, each of which reflects a different level of Divine emanation in the soul of the prophet:

- The letter *tzadik* corresponds to "mirror," reflecting the inner light that is contained in the rectified and righteous consciousness of all prophets.

- The letter *lamed* corresponds to "clear vision" as it appears in the revelation of the *chayah* (the second-highest level of the soul) in Aaron's relatively clear visions.

- The final *mem* corresponds "clear vision" as it appears in the revelation of the *yechidah* (the highest level of the soul) in Moses' absolutely clear visions.

The level of prophecy corresponding to *mareh* reflects both the *lamed* and the *mem*, the two highest levels of the soul (*chayah and yechidah*). These are the two surrounding lights that are generally inaccessible to one's inner consciousness.

level of prophecy	letter of *tzelem*	type of prophecy
"a mirror"	*tzadik*	all prophets
"clear vision"	*lamed*	Aaron
	final *mem*	Moses

For more on the different levels of the soul, see at length in *Anatomy of the Soul* and in our extended Hebrew volume, *Hanefesh*.

7. The Talmud states that the Torah was given through the combined energies of these three siblings, "Blessed is the Merciful One who gave a three-fold Torah [Torah, Prophets and Writings] to a three-fold nation [*Kohanim*, Levites and Israelites] by means of three [the three siblings (an alternate interpretation is, by means of the third-born, Moses)]" (*Shabbat* 88a).

The three siblings also correspond to the three pillars of our Divine service, each of which begins with the letter *tav*: Torah (תורה), prayer (תפלה), and repentance or return to God (תשובה). Moses, as the conduit through which God gave the Torah to His people, corresponds to Torah; Aaron, the High Priest, whose task was to stand before God in the Tabernacle and to serve Him through sacrifice and prayer, corresponds to prayer; and Miriam, who repented for speaking badly of her brother Moses, corresponds to repentance. The combined numerical value of these three Hebrew words is 1,839 (the exact value of the verse in Psalms 119:18, "Open my eyes that I may behold the wonders of Your Torah"), which equals 3 times 613, thus 613 is the average value of the three words.

The numerical value of the commonly used phrase "Moses, our teacher" (משה רבינו) is also 613, as is the number of commandments that the Jewish people are commanded to observe. All three siblings are thus encompassed in the all-inclusive soul of Moses, through whom God chose to give the Torah with its 613 commandments. The numerical value of the word *Torah* (תורה), corresponding to Moses, is only 611, however when we add the two commandments represented by Aaron and Miriam, the commandment to pray and the commandment to regret and correct our misdeeds, we reach 613!

The total numerical value of the names of the three siblings is 891, which is equal to the phrase "we will do and we will hear [i.e., comprehend]" (נעשה ונשמע), which the Jewish nation proclaimed at the revelation at Mt. Sinai. It is also the numerical value of the phrase, "the exodus from Egypt" (יציאת מצרים), which God effected in order to enable the Jewish nation to receive the Torah on Mt. Sinai.

When added together, 1,839 (the total value of *Torah, tefilah* and *teshuvah*) and 891 (the total value of the names of the three siblings) equal 2,730, which is also equal to 5 times the product of God's two essential Names, *Havayah* (26) and *Ekyeh* (21). In Kabbalah, these two Names correspond to the two supernal *sefirot* of wisdom and understanding. Wisdom corresponds to the revelation of God's continual, eternal Being (*Havayah*, short for "was, is, will be"), while understanding corresponds to the awareness of the World to Come, God's Being as will be revealed in the ultimate future (*Ekyeh*, "I will be"). The fact that 2,730 equals five times the product of these Names, reflects their manifestation in each of the five levels of consciousness of the soul (*nefesh, ruach, neshamah, chayah, yechidah,* as explained elsewhere).

8. While serving as midwives for the Jewish women in Egypt, Miriam (also called Puah) and her mother, Yocheved (Shifrah), refused to carry out Pharaoh's inhumane command to kill all the Jewish male

babies as they were born. As a reward for this courageous act, Miriam merited to be the forebearer of kings (see Rashi to Exodus 1:21). In Kabbalah, this reward is interpreted to mean that the soul of Miriam assists Jews looking to reconnect with their Judaism and future converts to Judaism in their quest for the truth, since both of these groups are connected to the *sefirah* of kingdom (as above, end of note 1).

9. There are nine verses that begin with the phrase "And God said." The tenth saying is the first verse of Genesis, "In the beginning..." (*Bartenura* on *Avot* 5:1). These ten sayings vitalize all existence at every moment and if, God forbid, He would ever decide to take back these sayings, the world would return to the initial state of nothingness at which it began, before the heavens and the earth were created (*Tanya, Sha'ar Hayichud Vehaemunah* ch. 1).

10. These three manifestations of the Hebrew letters correspond to the three horizontal divisions of the *sefirot*, as follows (see also *What You Need to Know About Kabbalah*, p.96; *The Hebrew Letters* pp. 2-3):

horizontal division	manifestation in the world	realm of manifestation in psyche	role of letters
wisdom, understanding and knowledge	mind and soul	intellectual powers	channels of consciousness
loving-kindness, might and beauty	organic matter	emotional powers	life-force
eternity, acknowledgment, foundation and kingdom	inorganic matter	behavioral powers	building blocks

It is strongly recommended that you to study in depth our book, *The Hebrew Letters—Channels of Divine Consciousness*, in which these ideas are dealt with in great depth.

11. The Hebrew word for ink (דיו), is a permutation of the full spelling of the letter *yud* (יוד). *Yud* is the letter with which the World to Come is created (*Menachot* 29b). Although the light of the World to Come is infinite and present at all times, the very fact that it is infinite makes it invisible to our finite eyes. This is the interpretation of the teaching that the Torah is "black fire written upon white fire" (*Yerushalmi Shekalim* 6:1). In order for the light of the letters to be revealed, the *yud* (יוד) with which the World to Come was created must permute into the black ink (דיו), which makes the Torah accessible to mankind (see *Likutei Torah, Shir Hashirim* 4b).

Another permutation of the same three letters is a word meaning "illness" (דוי). When visiting the sick, the Arizal tells us to have in mind the intention to transpose the letters of "illness" so that they spell *yud*, thus bringing the sick person respite by illuminating his world with the life-giving light of the World to Come.

12. When the Jewish people contemplate God, as it were, by studying His Torah, then God also perceives the Jewish people through the prism of the Torah, by which we appear to be infinitely big. This is the meaning of the verse, "Observe from Your holy abode, from the heavens and bless Your nation of Israel…" (Deuteronomy, 26:15). For when God looks down upon His nation of Israel from above and sees how they are serving Him through keeping the Torah and *mitzvot*, He sees them as one who observes something through a magnifying glass (see the Bar Mitzvah discourse, *Ita Bemidrash Tilim*).

13. *Shulchan Aruch, Even Ha'ezer* 8:5; *Mishneh Torah, Hilchot Issurei Biyah* 15:4.

14. See Rabbi Ben-Zion Meir Chai Uziel's, *Piskei Uziel, Bisheilot Hazman*, 61.

THE MEANING OF "THREE TIMES SEVEN"

I am not Jewish and this is awkward to ask, but I have had a burning question now for the past two years.

I had a dream in which I saw the face of a man whom I thought was J. but I heard a voice that said "No, this is Joshua, you may ask for one thing, but it cannot be material." I asked to see my deceased brother, even for fifteen seconds, and next I was on top of the whitest stairs I've ever seen and many people strolled at the bottom. When I looked I saw my brother smile at me, and then he was gone.

After this, I was in what appeared to be an old sanctuary with many candles. I felt a presence of the Messiah and I asked him "When are you returning?" And the voice replied, "Three times seven."

I have been told that in the Jewish faith numbers and letters have significant meanings. Some people say dreams are just dreams, but I would certainly like your opinion.

IN JEWISH TEACHINGS, the general rule concerning dreams is that "dreams speak in vain."[1] However, when straightforward, meaningful messages suggest themselves in dreams we may take note of them in order to improve our lives and become more spiritually connected.[2]

The sages teach us that "sleep is one-sixtieth of death"[3] meaning that, whereas in death, the soul departs from the body completely, in sleep it remains connected to the lower worlds to a large extent (fifty-nine parts out of sixty).

Yet, while we are asleep, a certain aspect of our soul rises to higher realms of consciousness than those which we are generally capable of reaching while awake. This explains why we may sometimes "meet" deceased souls in our dreams.[4]

In sleep the eyes are closed to outer reality. The power of sight, together with the other conscious powers of the mind and heart, disappear into their unconscious source. Although this source may reflect itself in dreams and other involuntary phenomena of sleep, these phenomena occur at the most external levels of the soul and, not being based upon objective sight, are unreal. [5] This is indicated by their lack of intrinsic order and consistency.

These phenomena are actually healthy and rejuvenating for the subsequent awakening as indicated by the root of the Hebrew word for "dream" (חלם), which also means soundness of health in general, and mental health in particular.[6]

An important feature of your dream is that the figure you saw identified himself as Joshua and not who you initially thought him to be (due to your upbringing as a believer in that individual).

The Joshua that you saw and heard most likely relates to the original Joshua of the Bible. Joshua was the greatest disciple of Moses and the leader of the Jewish people who, after the passing of Moses, brought the people into the Land of Israel, and then conquered and settled the land.[7]

When Moses left Egypt during the exodus of the Jewish nation, he took with him the bones of Joseph, Joshua's forbearer.[10] In Hebrew, the word for "bones" (עצמות) can also be read to mean "spiritual essence." In the future, Moses as the final redeemer will also bring with him the essence of Joseph/Joshua. With the coming of the Mashiach, both souls will join together in one person to bring the true and final redemption to the Jewish people and to all of humanity.[11]

So, Moses, as Joshua's spiritual mentor, is the archetypal soul of Israel who redeems the nation from exile and bondage. In fact, it is also Moses who will return to become the final redeemer (i.e., the

Moses, Joshua and King David (together with his son and successor, King Solomon) all appear in one context as the authors of the three principal passages in the blessing made after meals (ברכת המזון).[8] This suggests that the grace after meals, the one blessing explicitly mandated by Moses in the Torah,[9] is a truly messianic commandment. To thank and bless God for the physical and spiritual sustenance that He bestows upon us creates in our consciousness the vessel in which the Mashiach—the ultimate goodness to all of creation for which reason God created the world—can reveal himself.

Mashiach). In the words of the sages, "He [Moses] was the original redeemer, and he shall [return to] be the final redeemer."[12] Joshua, as his name implies,[13] is the archetypal soul who saves the nation from its enemies by bringing them to their land.[14] So, while Moses is the redeemer, Joshua is the savior.[15]

Furthermore, while the **soul** of the Mashiach is identified with that of Moses, the **spiritual garment** of Mashiach's soul, (which gives him the ability to express his inner spiritual powers in thought, word and deed), is identified with Joshua. Similarly, the **body** of the Mashiach (the manner in which he appears to the outside world, his aura of authority and sovereignty and his general character) is identified with King David, of who the Mashiach will be a physical descendant. Thus, the Mashiach figure is truly a composite of these three archetypal souls: Moses, Joshua and David—the redeemer, the savior, and the king.[16]

Joshua is a descendent of Joseph and is considered to be his reincarnation.[17] Often the sages speak of two messianic figures, Mashiach the son of Joseph and Mashiach the son of David.[18] Maimonides[19] and Chassidic teachings[20] explain that these two figures are simultaneously present in the one, true Mashiach, but express themselves in two different stages of his revelation to the world (first, the Mashiach the son of Joseph and then, the Mashiach the son of David). In addition, the *Zohar* speaks of a third messianic figure, "the faithful shepherd," who will appear (in the one Mashiach) after the Mashiach the son of Joseph and the Mashiach the son of David. This third messianic figure refers to the return of Moses, another part of the composite soul of the Mashiach discussed above.[21]

To explain this idea further, while the essence of Jewish faith is in the absolute oneness of God,[22] much of Jewish identity is based on the principle of "three."[23] In addition to the three spiritual elements contained within the Mashiach, as described above, the Jewish people originate from three Patriarchs—three soul-roots—Abraham, Isaac and Jacob, and we address our daily prayers to "our God and the God of our fathers; the God of Abraham, the God of Isaac and the God of Jacob."[24]

Having discussed the issue of three and how it pertains to Joshua, we will now see how the seven of your riddle relates to the matter. For a non-Jew, spiritual rectification involves the refinement of the seven innate emotive attributes of his soul through the observance of the seven commandments mandated by the Torah for all humanity. These are called the Seven Laws of Noah and include prohibitions against murder, adultery, theft, idolatory, blasphemy, and eating the flesh of a live animal, plus a mandate to establish a just legal system.[25]

In nature, the number seven also reflects the division of light into the seven colors of the rainbow. The number seven is thus particularly connected to the natural phenomena in our world, and alludes to the covenant between God and Noah (the covenant of the rainbow), and thus to the seven Laws of Noah.[26]

With the era of redemption, the rectified "three" of Jewish consciousness will unite with the rectified "seven" of non-Jewish consciousness to bear spiritual offspring ("be fruitful and multiply,"[27] multiplication being a more powerful function than addition). Mathematically, this translates into "three times seven,"[28] the riddle of your dream. The offspring that will exude from this union is the true recognition of all of humanity that "God is one." This recognition will usher in the messianic age, when all peoples will serve God together.

Study the information for righteous gentiles on our website and in our book *Kabbalah and Meditation for the Nations*, and may God bless you and your children with all things good. Remember that God watches over all of His creations, and certainly over all human beings.

May your life be filled with love and joy!

With blessings of the Torah and the Land of Israel,

Notes:

1. Zachariah 10:2; *Berachot* 55b.

2. In the Bible there are numerous accounts of dreams that were significant and even prophetic. The Talmud states that whereas sleep is considered one-sixtieth of death, dreams are considered to be one-sixtieth of prophecy (*Berachot* 57b). Also take note of the Talmudic dictum which states, "Just as there is no grain without straw, so there is no dream without superfluous matter" (*Berachot* 55b). Even if a dream appears to be of some importance, not all the symbols in the dream will necessarily be significant.

In dreams, the power of imagination takes the form of physical actions and imagery. However, this is the manifestation of the lowest, most external level of thought: "action within thought." Above this level are two other levels of thought: "thought within thought" and "speech within thought." Thought within thought is the deep awareness of an idea before one becomes conscious of letters of thought. Speech within thought (הרהור) is thought in the form of letters and words. See *Igeret Hakodesh* ch. 19, page 257.

3. *Berachot* 57b.

4. Even so, one must avoid doing certain acts to intentionally bring about such a rendezvous with the deceased (see table in letter 1, note 1 above, the explanation of Maimonides to "one who consults the dead").

5. See note 2, above.

6. See Radak, *Sefer Hashorashim*, (חל״מ).

7. See Joshua, chapter 1.

8. Rabbi Shneur Zalman of Liadi, *Shulchan Aruch Harav*, 187:2-3.

9. Deuteronomy 8:10.

10. Exodus 13:19.

11. *Zohar, Ra'aya Meheimna* 253b.

12. *Zohar* II, 120a.

13. In the original Hebrew, the letters of the name Joshua (יהושע) permute to spell the word for "salvation" (ישועה). For this reason, the name Joshua carries with it the implication of "savior." Literally, the name Joshua means "God saves."

14. Before crossing the Jordan, Joshua told the people to prepare their weapons for war. The verse then continues, "You are crossing this Jordan to come to inherit the land which GOD your God is giving to you as an inheritance" (Joshua 1:11; see Rashi's commentary on the verse). Later, while they were standing in the River Jordan (after it had miraculously split), Joshua reminded the people that the purpose for which they are crossing the Jordan is in order to disinherit the nations of the Land as we are commanded in the

Torah. If they accept this purpose, then well and good, however, if they do not accept it then the waters of the Jordan will come and drown them (*Sotah* 34a). This implies that the power to save the people from all its enemies is latent in their intention to conquer and settle the land, even as they first enter it.

15. The different roles played by Moses and Joshua are exemplified in the war of Israel against its archenemy, Amalek (Exodus 17:8-13), during which Moses (the redeemer), beseeches God in prayer ["Redemption must be juxtaposed to prayer" (*Berachot* 9b)], while Joshua (the savior), leads the Jewish army in battle, thus saving the people from the attack of its archenemy on the physical plane.

16. See our book in Hebrew *Sod Hashem Liyreiyav*, pp. 359-361. There the second component of the Messianic triad, in place of Joshua, is considered to be Jacob himself.

17. See Rabbi Chaim Vital, *Sha'ar Hagilgulim*, introduction 36.

18. The era of Messianic rectification is divided into two. The first stage of this era is personified by the figure of Joseph, and it culminates in the union of Torah and science. In Kabbalah, this is referred to as the union of the higher waters and the lower waters. This stage precedes the final stage of rectification, indicated by the full revelation of the Mashiach, now personified by the figure of King David, who will build the third, eternal Temple, revealing himself as the true leader for whom the world has waited (see *Rectifying the State of Israel*, ch. 13-14).

19. In his *Mishneh Torah* (*Hilchot Melachim* ch. 11), Maimonides mentions only one Mashiach who will be "a king from the House of David." This does not contradict his ruling (*Hilchot Melachim* ch. 1) that a king of Israel (not the Mashiach) may be from any of the tribes of Israel.

20. See *Likutei Sichot*, volume 32, Appendices, *Nisan*, 185.

21. See *Zohar* III, *Ra'aya Meheimna* 253b; *Zohar* I 25b. The root of the soul of Moses, who appears as the final revelation of the Mashiach, is indeed higher than both of the first two. Only a soul from a source as

high as that of Moses' soul is able to bring the innermost secrets of the Torah into the world as if they are not secrets at all.

In Kabbalah and Chassidut it is explained that the soul-roots of Moses, Joseph and David that combine in the person of the Mashiach, derive from the three higher *sefirot* (supernal lights through which God created the world):

- the superconscious crown (the root of Moses in the Mashiach)
- wisdom (the root of David in the Mashiach)
- understanding (the root of Joseph/Joshua in the Mashiach)

These three messianic figures come to redeem, save and rule over the seven lower *sefirot* that define reality as we know it.

The world was created in six days, and God rested on the seventh (Genesis, chapter 1). The complete cycle of seven days corresponds to the seven emotive and active powers of the soul (loving-kindness, might, beauty, victory, acknowledgment, foundation and kingdom). It is the function of the three higher, transcendent *sefirot* to rectify the seven lower *sefirot* by shining their light and energy into each one of them individually.

In this constellation of *sefirot*, Moses appears on the center axis, David on the right and Joseph on the left. This appears to differ from the way in which they appear in the lower *sefirot*, with Moses on the right (victory, the branch of loving-kindness) and both Joseph and David in the center (Joseph in foundation and David in kingdom). This is because, as taught in Kabbalah, the superconscious crown is the ultimate source of victory in the soul (in Hebrew, the word for, "victory" (נצח), also means "eternity," as manifest in its source); wisdom (on the right) is the source of kingdom; and understanding (on the left) is the source of foundation.

22. The essential proclamation of faith that a Jew declares twice every day, morning and evening, is the verse, "Hear O' Israel, GOD is our God, GOD is one!" (Deuteronomy 6:4).

23. In general, the number three represents equilibrium and stability as is expressed in the *Mishnah*, "The world stands upon three things, upon the Torah, upon prayer and upon kind deeds" (*Avot* 1:2).

   The Jewish people as a whole are divided into three groups: *Kohanim* (priests), *Leviim* (Levites) and *Yisraelim* (Israelites). See also, Letter 12, note 7.

24. The *Amidah* prayer, which is recited three times a day on a normal weekday (see any Jewish prayerbook). The three patriarchs correspond to the first three of the lower *sefirot*; the emotive attributes of the heart: loving-kindness (Abraham), might (Isaac) and beauty (Jacob). The first two of these three character traits are balanced in direct contrast to one another (in the body they correspond to the right and the left hands), while the third (which corresponds to the body, the torso, itself) represents the power to unify the two and enables them to generate "offspring" in the form of the *sefirot* below them (see our book in Hebrew, *Sod Hashem Liyreiyav*, pp. 46-48).

25. For more on the seven Noahide commandments, see our book, *Kabbalah and Meditation for the Nations*.

   If a non-Jew neglects his or her obligation to observe these seven commandments, he or she remains unable to comprehend God's true unity and is liable to fall into idolatry.

26. For a detailed discussion about patterns of 3 and 7, see *Kabbalah and Meditation for the Nations* pp. 62ff.

27. Genesis 1:28.

28. 3 times 7 equals 21, the numerical value of the Divine Name *Ekyeh*. *Ekyeh* is the Name by which God revealed Himself to Moses at the Burning Bush when He charged him with the mission of redeeming the Jewish people from Egypt.

   For more on the significance of the various Divine Names, see our book *What You Need to Know About Kabbalah*, Ch. 9.

LETTER 14

RASHBI IN A DREAM

I am writing regarding a dream I had a week ago. In it, Rashbi[1] *came to tell me something. I did not actually see him, but rather was aware of his presence. It was as though I was dreaming that I was dreaming. I protested to him, saying that I would not remember what he was telling me when I woke up. But he reassured me that when I ask for an interpretation of the dream, the interpreter will be able to tell me exactly what he,* Rashbi, *had said.*

BEFORE ATTEMPTING to shed light on your dream, let us note that in the Bible the two greatest dream interpreters are Joseph and Daniel. Each solved the dream of a king: Joseph solved Pharaoh's dreams and Daniel solved Nebuchadnezzar's dream. Pharaoh recalled his dreams and told them to Joseph, who was left to convey to Pharaoh what God had in store for Egypt and the world by correctly interpreting the dreams.[2] But Nebuchadnezzar forgot his dream,[3] and Daniel had to reconstruct the dream from nothing (similar to the act of creating something from nothing[4]) and then interpret its meaning! God revealed to Daniel both the dream and its interpretation.[5]

In the case of your dream, in one respect it is similar to the Pharaoh-Joseph scenario, but in another respect it is like the Nebuchadnezzar-Daniel scenario. We know that you dreamt about Rabbi Shimon bar Yochai (*Rashbi*), unlike Daniel, who knew absolutely nothing about the content of Nebuchadnezzar's dream, but the essence of the message of the dream remains unknown. What did *Rashbi* say to you?! We seem to be left without an inkling!

However, knowing that you dreamt about *Rashbi*, and that he told you that the interpreter of your dream would surely know what he had said, suggests that his message relates to the essence of his soul and to his mission on earth, to that which was (and is) more dear to him than all: revealing the teachings of the *Zohar* to the world. In the *Zohar* we find that Moses[6] told *Rashbi* that the true and complete redemption with the coming of the Mashiach, in a manner of love and mercy, depends upon the revelation of the secrets of the *Zohar*.[7]

In order to better understand *Rashbi*'s mission on earth, it is important to note his place in history:

From the time of the revelation of the Torah at Mt. Sinai, the secrets of the Torah that today we call Kabbalah were known only to the priests and the prophets. However, after prophecy ceased and the Temple in Jerusalem was destroyed, it was *Rashbi* who was given the power and permission from

Heaven to reveal the inner wisdom of the Torah to his disciples.

Rashbi introduced and explained the most basic Kabbalistic model of the ten *sefirot*, which are the emanations of Divine light or energy that lie at the heart of all creation. His teachings are contained in his great classic text of Kabbalah, the *Zohar*.[8]

Some 1,500 years later, the Chassidic movement, headed by Rabbi Israel Ba'al Shem Tov, took the abstract and often impenetrable teachings of classic Kabbalah and the *Zohar* and recast them into the descriptive language and experiences of the human psyche and soul, thereby making them accessible even to the layman.[9]

Since in your dream you protested that you would not remember *Rashbi*'s own words to you, after which he told you that you would understand it through an interpreter, there is no better interpreter than *Rashbi* himself! And so, it would be advisable for you to learn the ways of *Rashbi* according to Chassidic teachings. For example, you might learn the *Zohar* with the Chassidic interpretations of the Alter Rebbe, the Mittler Rebbe, and the Tzemach Tzedek.

Rashbi wanted his teachings to be made known to all, for as mentioned above, only so will the redemption come with love and mercy. One should surely have this in mind when studying the *Zohar*. In general, the sages instruct us to have the welfare of others in mind when studying Torah. Torah is the ultimate energy and life source that can and should always be tapped to benefit mankind. When Torah is studied with the welfare of others in mind, it is referred to as the "Torah of loving-kindness,"[10] which the sages interpret to mean Torah that one studies in order to teach.[11] This is especially important in our generation with regard to Kabbalah and Chassidut, which reveal the inner dimension of the Torah, for this is the Divine wisdom that most touches the soul and arouses one to return to God and the way of the Torah.

Another important facet of your dream is that you knew that you were dreaming. At the end of our extended exile, just prior to the appearance of the Mashiach, the Psalmist says, "we were as dreamers."[12] While in exile, the Divine spark of the Jewish soul is in a state of sleep, and we will only become aware of it with the onset of the redemption.[13] In our present generation, just before the final redemption, the time is ripe to become fully aware of the fact that the exile is in fact a dream (a nightmare!) from which we must awaken. In the Song of Songs we read, "I am asleep, yet my heart is awake,"[14] which the sages interpret to mean that although I am asleep in exile, my heart is awake and beating strongly in anticipation of the imminent redemption.

The exile of the Jewish soul—the apparent loss of Jewish identity—is compared to a state of sleep. In sleep the eyes are closed to outer reality. The power of sight, together with the other conscious powers of mind and heart, disappear into their subconscious source. Although this source may reflect itself in dreams and other involuntary phenomena of sleep, these phenomena occur at the most external levels of the soul and, not being based upon objective perception, are unreal.

This is indicated by their lack of intrinsic order and consistency.

However, just as the Divine Presence never leaves the Western Wall, the one remaining wall of the Temple courtyard, even though the Temple itself has been destroyed, so too, there is a point within the heart of every Jew that is alive and burning even when he is empty of any other external Jewish characteristics, God forbid. This is the deeper meaning of the verse, "I am asleep..." mentioned above. The Jewish soul cries out, "although I may seem to be sleeping from *mitzvot*, my heart is awake to perform acts of loving-kindness..."[15] Elsewhere, the Midrash explains, "I am asleep [unaware] of the end [of the exile] but my heart is awake to the redemption."[16]

Thus the spark of inseparable connection to God that is hidden deep in the subconscious of the exiled soul can never be extinguished. Neither does it sleep, for it is ever ready to emerge from hiding upon hearing the call to return to God. The innermost point in the heart of the Jew, unlike the other powers of the soul, which may fall into a temporary state of slumber, is always awake at its source. There it beats in continuous motions of "run and return," running out to the unity of God and returning inward, into the separate reality of the self, in order to fulfill the Divine will and purpose of life. As the heart of a person sleeping continues to beat, so does the heart of every Jew continue to beat during this last, most dark and painful exile.[17]

To conclude, we will add a few words about one who sees or feels the presence of a *tzadik* in his dreams, which in itself is certainly a great privilege.

As pointed out above, the first thing on which to focus in trying to understand the meaning of the dream is the holy nature of the *tzadik* and his message to the world.[18] One should try to relate all of the details of the dream to the true nature of the *tzadik* in life.[19] This makes the dream real, for the righteous are always alive here on earth, and their work continues even after they appear to have left us.

In a letter sent to the residents of the Holy Land to console them after the passing of the *tzadik* Rebbe Menachem Mendel of Vitebsk, the Alter Rebbe (author of the *Tanya*) quotes the idiom used by the sages to describe the passing from this world, "He has left life for all living." The Alter Rebbe explains this to mean that every departed soul, especially the soul of a *tzadik*, has left something of his own life in this world for those who remain alive here. With regard to the *tzadik*, this is because even during his life on earth he lives in the spiritual worlds through his service of faith, love and awe. Thus, during his lifetime, the *tzadik* brings these highest spiritual levels into this world in his physical body, and his disciples are able to receive the emanations of these attributes by being in his presence and hearing his words and thoughts. After his passing, however, a certain part of the soul of the *tzadik* remains in this world, freed of the boundaries of his body, allowing his followers and disciples to connect to even more essential spiritual aspects of the *tzadik* than they were able to connect during his lifetime. The extent to which the person experiences this depends on the level of his connection to the *tzadik* during his lifetime.[20]

In addition, the sages teach us that seeing a *tzadik* in a dream often relates to the meaning of his name or allusions contained in its root or letters.[21] In relation to *Rashbi*, his proper name, *Shimon*, comes from the Hebrew root "to hear" or "to understand," the root of the word that begins our declaration of faith in one God: "Hear O Israel...." In affirming our faith verbally at least twice a day we may have in mind *Rashbi* and his teachings and his way of understanding God's absolute unity, as taught in the *Zohar*. In addition, in Hebrew, the letters of Shimon (שמעון) permute to spell, "there is a humble soul" (יש ענו), alluding to the fact that *Rashbi* is known in Kabbalah to have been the reincarnation of Moses, whom the Torah praises as being, "very humble."[22] It is Moses who says to Israel, "Hear O Israel, GOD is our God, GOD is one."[23]

With blessings of the Torah and the Land of Israel,

Many ask the question, does the tzadik who appears to me in a dream know that I am dreaming about him and does he actually control or direct the dream. The answer to this question is complex. In general, the answer is: not necessarily.

The following stories illustrate this point.

Once a young boy was very ill, so much so that his parents feared for his life. The father traveled to a Rebbe who lived in the next town and told him of his son's illness, asking him to pray for the child. When the father returned home, the child was still in mortal danger, however the parents were somewhat relieved from their worry because they knew that the *tzadik* would pray for the child. That evening a well-respected doctor from a nearby town knocked at their door and asked if there was someone in the house who was ill. In great surprise, the parents led the doctor to the child's bedside, and the doctor proceeded to treat him. With the doctor's help, the child soon recovered from his illness.

The parents asked the doctor what had brought him to their house on that day, and he replied that the night before the *tzadik* had appeared to him in a dream and had beseeched him to go to their house and treat the patient.

The father traveled once again to the Rebbe to thank him for his supernatural intervention, however, when he related the doctor's words, the Rebbe replied that he had done nothing more than pray for the child's wellbeing.

Another story is told about the Lubavitcher Rebbe who once appeared to someone in a dream. The next morning, the person stood outside the Rebbe's home and pondered whether or not the dream had been a true dream and whether or not the Rebbe was conscious of his appearance to him in his dream. As he stood outside, the Rebbe passed by, and with a smile, whispered, "Dreams speak of naught." [Note that from this story we cannot know for sure what the answer to our question is!]

Notes:

1. *Rashbi* is the acronym for **Rabbi Shimon Bar Yochai**, a first century sage.

2. Genesis 41:1-30. Joseph interpreted two consecutive dreams that Pharaoh dreamt on the same night. In the first dream, Pharaoh saw seven fat cows consumed by seven lean cows, with no apparent change occurring in the seven lean cows. In the second dream, Pharaoh saw seven plump ears of grain growing on one stalk followed by seven scrawny and meager stalks which swallowed up the seven plump ears of grain. Joseph interpreted these dreams to mean that Egypt would be blessed with seven years of plenty followed by seven years of famine.

3. All that he remembered was that he had dreamt a terrifying dream. See note 5 below.

4. To reconstruct "something from nothing" (i.e., from no substantial evidence of what the "something" might be) relates to the manner in which the World of Action, the lowest and most physical of the four spiritual worlds, is created.

In Kabbalah it is explained that the entire Book of Daniel pertains to the rectification of this lowest world, achieved by reconstructing its spiritual state from an apparent absence of spirituality (spiritual "nothingness"). Since in general, dreams reflect the relatively spiritual aspect of this world, in order for Daniel to accomplish this rectification, he had to reach the true, Divine "nothing" (not in the sense of being unknown to us but rather in the sense of being essentially unknowable to finite consciousness) of the World of Emanantion and draw its consciousness down into the World of Action. In the words of the Magid of Mezritch, Daniel revealed that "*Atzilut* [the exclusively spiritual consciousness of the World of Emanation] is here too."

In contrast, Joseph's interpretation of Pharaoh's dream was an act of creating "something from something." Relative to Daniel and Nebuchadnezzar, Joseph and Pharaoh were in the World of Formation, the world where "something" is created from "something" (i.e., from a known source [from the World of Creation, the world above the World of Formation]). Having successfully interpreted Pharaoh's dream, Joseph went on to suggest to Pharaoh that he hoard enough produce during the seven years of plenty to last during the seven years of famine. He also suggested that a viceroy be appointed to oversee this process. Pharaoh recognized that there was no better candidate for this position than Joseph himself. Thus in a short moment, Joseph metamorphosed from an imprisoned and convicted slave into second-in-command to the king of Egypt. Pharaoh recognized that in order for Joseph to have interpreted his dreams correctly (which he and his servants felt intuitively, even before the dream and its interpretation became manifest in reality), he must have been inspired by the "spirit of God." But Pharaoh did not make the mistake of worshiping Joseph as a god. In contrast, Nebuchadnezzar, totally astonished by Daniel's ability to reconstruct his dream from nothing, began to worship him.

The reason why the World of Action appears to come from nothing more than the World of Formation is the secret of the word *af* (literally, "even"), which appears in the verse that most directly pertains to the relationship between the four worlds: "All that is called by **My Name** [referring to the World of Emanation;], I have **created** it [the World of Creation], I have **formed** it [the World of Formation], even have I **made** it [the World of Action]." In this verse, the word "even" (אף) divides between the World of Action and the three higher worlds. In Chassidut, this separation of the worlds is identified as the cause of the apparent absence of Divinity in this world. For this reason it is here that the non-Jewish soul is liable to fall into idolatry, which arouses God's wrath (חרון אף), another Hebrew idiom that contains the word אף (see Maimonides, *Guide to the Perplexed*, 1:36, that in the Torah, the expression חרון אף always refers to sins of idolatry).

In Pharaoh's dream, the phrase that is used to describe his spontaneous reaction upon awakening is "his spirit was troubled" (ותפעם רוחו; Genesis 41:8). With Nebuchadnezzar, a similar but slightly different phrase (ותתפעם רוחו), using the reflective form of the verb, is used (Daniel 2:1). ותפעם has only one letter *tav*, while ותתפעם has two. Rashi explains that the difference is that with regard to Pharaoh, only the interpretation of his dream was concealed from him, while with regard to Nebuchadnezzar both the dream itself and its interpretation were concealed. Another difference noted by the sages is that, in Joseph's case, Pharaoh's dream was in order to bring greatness upon one person (Joseph), whereas in the case of Daniel, there were four people who received greatness as a result of Nebuchadnezzar's dream: Daniel, Chananyah, Mishael and Azariah (*Bereishit Rabah, Parshat Vayeshev*, 49:5).

5. Daniel ch. 2. King Nebuchadnezzar dreamt a terrifying nightmare. Upon awakening, he forgot the dream but was still sorely troubled by it. He commanded his magicians to either relate the dream to him, together with its interpretation, or suffer death. Daniel prayed fervently that God assist him and save himself and his companions from death. During the night Daniel had a vision of Nebuchadnezzar's dream. He returned to the king the following morning and told him how God had assisted him in revealing the dream and its interpretation. Nebuchadnezzar subsequently appointed Daniel to rule over Babylonia and all of its wise men.

6. One of the books of the *Zohar* is called *Ra'aya Meheimna* ("Faithful Shepherd"), referring to Moses who appeared to *Rashbi* and related the content of this composition.

7. The *Zohar* states that until the time of the redemption, the influence of the Tree of Knowledge of Good and Evil will dominate the world. However, with the redemption, that dominance will be referred to the Tree of Life. Those people who studied and internalized the mystical teachings of the Tree of Life as they appear in the *Zohar* will not be put to the test that will be given to those who studied only the revealed parts of the Torah that deal with the separation of good from evil, permitted from forbidden, etc. (*Ra'aya Meheimna, Naso*). See also, *Tanya, Igeret Hakodesh,* ch. 26.

8. *Zohar* means "splendor," or "brilliance."

9. See *What You Need to Know About Kabbalah,* pp. 4-11.

10. Proverbs 31:26.

11. *Sukah* 49b.

12. Psalms 121:1.

13. *Torah Or*, 28c-29a.

14. Song of Songs, 5:2.

15. *Hayom Yom*, 21 *Tamuz*.

16. *Yalkut Shimoni, Shir Hashirim,* 5.

17. See at length in, *I am Asleep Yet My Heart is Awake*.

18. Every *tzadik* has a special mission and a special message to the world. Also, just as "no two prophets prophecy with the same style of expression" (*Sanhedrin* 89a), so too, every *tzadik* has a special style through which he transmits his message to the world.

19. The Talmud (*Berachot* 57b) offers interpretations for many examples of dreams in which a person or a written name appears. For example, one who sees King Solomon, the wisest of all men, in a dream, should look forward to wisdom as should one who sees Rebbe or ben Zomah in a dream. One who sees King David or Rabbi Elazar ben Azariah or ben Azai, who were all notably pious, in a dream, should expect piety. However, one who sees King Ahab (an evil king), Rabbi Yishmael ben Elisha (who was unmercifully tortured to death by the Romans), or Acher (Elisha ben Avuyah, who became an heretic), should be wary of impending danger, taking care to improve his behavior in order to avert it. It should be noted that in each case, the good interpretations are based on the qualities of the people seen in the dream, while the bad interpretation of the person's appearance in the dream is either because of his Heavenly ordained fate or because he succumbed to the wiles of his own evil inclination.

20. *Igeret Hakodesh* ch. 27.

21. The Talmud (*Berachot* 56b) offers some examples of this phenomenon, for instance, one who sees a person whose name is Huna in a dream will experience a miracle, while if a person called Chaninah, Chananyah, or Yochanan, appears to him in a dream, the dreamer will experience a number of miracles. This interpretation is based on the letter *nun* [the initial letter of "miracle" (נס) which appears in the name Huna and is doubled in the other three names (Rashi)], all of which stem from the root, "to be graced" (חנן). Another example is that one who sees dates (תמר) in a dream, is being told that his sins have ended (תמו עוונתיו), i.e., have been atoned for, as in the verse "Your sin has ended [תם], daughter of Zion" (Lamentations

4:22). (See also, Letter 11, referring to the Aramaic names for cat, *shinra* or *shunra*.)

Indeed, understanding the meaning of the Hebrew words and letters is the most important key to dream interpretation, the talent of Joseph, the archetypal dream interpreter, as explained in Letter 11, note 23.

Sometimes the interpretation of a dream concerns events that happened to the person who appears in it. For example, the Talmud relates that if one sees Pinchas, who, in his zealous deed against the act of Zimri and Kozbi (Numbers, ch. 25), had many wonders occur for him, as we are taught in the midrash, so too, the dreamer can expect similar wonders to occur for him (Rashi; in this case the interpretation is also related to the letters of Pinchas' name).

Another important rule that we learn from the Talmud, is that upon awakening one should relate the dream to a verse that refers positively to the content of the dream. One example of this, mentioned above, is seeing dates in a dream. Similarly if one sees a grapevine in a dream one should relate it to the verse, "Your wife is like a fertile vine..." (Psalms 128:3). If one sees olive trees in a dream one should relate it to the verse, "Your children are like the saplings of olives around your table" (*ibid.* 128:4).

Since dreams follow the spoken interpretation that is given them (see *Berachot* 55b), if one dreams a dream that troubles him, he should relate it to three friends who, upon hearing the dream, should reply, "You have dreamt a good dream." In addition, there are nine verses from the Bible which his friends should recite. Three of the verses relate to occasions in which God turned evil into good, three of them relate to occasions in which God released people from captivity and the last three verses relate to peace.

22. Numbers 12:3.

23. Deuteronomy 6:4.

A BRILLIANT LIGHT

I have made it my habit to learn after midnight on Shabbat night to pay God back for time not spent studying and to give thanks for everything. I learn the Zohar, and one particular night, as I held the book in my hands, I nodded off for a few seconds. During those first few seconds I saw a beautiful light that I have never ever seen before; its brilliance was outstanding white and rays of colors. I nodded off again for a few seconds, and I saw a hand place notes of money into my wallet. I am left wondering about this fabulous light that I saw and experienced.

BEFORE WE ATTEMPT to give meaning to your experience, let us begin with a few introductory words that will place your experience in its proper perspective. The foundation of Judaism is to be sincere and wholehearted in all our actions,[1] and to believe that all that transpires is by the hand of Divine Providence. The more we wholeheartedly and sincerely connect to God, the more joy we experience in our lives.[2]

With the coming of the Mashiach, who will raise universal consciousness to a level yet unknown,[3] every event in our lives—every breath,[4] every motion[5]—will be experienced as a miracle. The continual re-creation of the universe,[6] the miracle underlying all reality, will become apparent to the physical eye.

Since the flow of miracles will be continuous, they will not be experienced as a novelty. On the one hand, we will retain a deep experience of the miracle and the wonder of the presence of God, while on the other hand, miracles will become nature. Not only will this perspective not prevent us from progressing in our service and consciousness of God, it will actually aid us in endlessly ascending from level to level.[7]

Since we are clearly approaching the time of the Mashiach,[8] we must already begin to live in the consciousness of the messianic age.[9] This means that we should live in a consciousness that each event that happens is indeed miraculous. This perception should not hinder us in our way of life; rather it should motivate us to continue to strive to reach ever higher levels in our service and consciousness of God. Even so, over-deliberating about any particular experience is liable to hinder the momentum by causing us to become involved in an egoistical debate about the nature of our experience and its significance, instead of allowing us to continue our service of God in true simplicity.

From all the above, we learn that we should accustom ourselves to relate naturally to even the most incredible and extraordinary experiences and to utilize them correctly for our spiritual advance.

From this perspective, we can now turn to your experience on Shabbat night.[10] Firstly, your desire to give thanks to God for everything is the simple meaning of the *sefirah* of acknowledgement.[11] Thanksgiving is the first and foremost interpretation of the *sefirah* of acknowledgement (הוד) and is the most fundamental quality necessary for achieving rectified character traits. Expressing thanks depends upon the person's level of holistic simplicity and sincerity (the inner experience of the *sefirah* of acknowledgement); the extent to which he sees the value of the simple things in life and to which his life is clear of imagined necessities. By being content and happy with the fulfillment of his basic needs, a person naturally wishes to offer honest thanks to whoever bestows goodness upon him.

Concerning the brilliant light that you saw when you nodded off the first time, you probably know that the word *Zohar*, the name of the classic text of Kabbalah, written by Rabbi Shimon bar Yochai almost 2,000 years ago, means "brilliance." There are thirteen synonyms for "light" in the Torah, which correspond to the thirteen principles of Divine mercy, the source of forgiveness, and the channels through which the super-conscious mind becomes revealed to the conscious mind. According to the Kabbalistic order of these synonyms, *Zohar*, "brilliant light," is the third of the thirteen, and thus corresponds to the third principle of Divine mercy, "He who pardons."[12]

The hand that placed notes of money into your wallet can be understood to allude to the "four hundred silver shekels" with which Abraham purchased the Machpela cave from Efron.[15] In Kabbalah it is explained that these four hundred silver shekels symbolize four hundred worlds of brilliant-silver light that will be inherited by the righteous in the World to Come[16] (safely deposited in your wallet for the time being!).

The verse states, "For they will see eye to eye when GOD returns to Zion".[13] The numerical value of the entire verse is 1,001 which equals 13 times 77. The combined numerical value of the initial letters of each word in this phrase together with the final letters of each word equals 377 which is once again a product of 13 (13 times 29), while the remaining intermediate letters equal 624 (13 times 48). Three separate words in the phrase are divisible by 26 (2 times 13): "eye" (עין; 130), Havayah (God's essential Name; 26), and "Zion" (ציון; 156), where the two words עין הוי together equal ציון.

The number 13 alludes to the revelation of the thirteen mazalot of "the holy beard," from which emanates the great compassion of the sefirah of the superconscious crown. As the numerical value of the word מזל equals 77, so the entire verse, 1,001, contains 13 mazalot. These are the channels by which the super-conscious is revealed to the conscious mind.[14]

Four hundred is also the numerical value of the word meaning "erudite" (משכיל). This term appears in the verse in the Book of Daniel which states, "And the erudite will glow like the brilliance [זהר] of the heavens;"[17] the very verse from which the name of the Zohar is taken.

The fact that you nodded off twice, each time for a few seconds and each time with a different experience/vision, reflects the two basic stages of any complete spiritual experience, referred to as "run and return."[18] The "run" is a totally spiritual experience, an experience of pure light. The "return" is an experience of the light manifesting in a more real and tangible way, in this case as notes of money placed into your wallet. In the psyche a healthy balance must be achieved between the soul's tendency to "run" out towards God, and, in danger of departing from the body, the need to "return" to physical reality.[19]

May God bless you in all areas of your life, with children, good health and abundance! The main thing is to persist in your study of the Torah and in the fulfillment of its commandments and to wholeheartedly serve God with joy!

With blessings of the Torah and the Land of Israel,

Notes:

1. See Deuteronomy 18:13. See at length in Letter 1 and also Letter 7, note 5. Rashi explains this verse to mean, "Walk with Him wholeheartedly and wait for Him. Do not investigate future forecasts, rather, all that happens to you accept wholeheartedly, and then you will be with Him, and will be His portion."

    The points Rashi makes in his interpretation correspond to the words of the verse. They can also be corresponded to the letters of God's essential Name (*Havayah*) as follows:

correspondence with letter from *Havayah*	word in verse	Rashi's commentary
tip of *yud*	תמים wholehearted	walk with Him in wholeheartedly
yud	תהיה be	and wait for Him
hei	עם with	do not investigate future broadcasts
vav	הוי' GOD	all that happens to you accept wholeheartedly
hei	א-להיך your God	then, you will be with Him, and will be His portion

For a detailed study of this correspondence, see our book in Hebrew, *Sod Hashem Liyreiav*, pp.450-455.

A detailed explanation of Rashi's interpretation of this verse is found in the commentary of the Rebbe of Komarna, *Heichal Habrachah*. The following table outlines his explanation:

word in verse	Rashi's commentary	*Heichal Habrachah*
תמים whole-hearted	walk with Him wholeheartedly	do not ponder about God's actions. Have the simple faith of a day-old babe that the Master of the Universe is present in every movement and nothing, whether large or small, happens by coincidence. Be happy and joyful that you are a Jew and devote every action to God.

תהיה be	and wait for Him	by living with the Torah and its commandments, the true source of all vitality, a person feels that he is being renewed and revived at every moment and that all the worries of the world around him are of no consequence, for he reveals the richest meaning of life. By living in this way he will know that there is no existence whatsoever besides God and that He is with him in even the darkest of times.
עם with	do not investigate future broadcasts	the word עם is the secret of *Gan Eden* (Paradise). Nonetheless, even though this is so, do not try to calculate whether or not your deeds earn you a place in the World to Come, rather serve God through love and fear, in joy and simplicity and without vice.
הוי׳ GOD	all that happens to you accept wholeheartedly	By accepting everything that happens in this world with love, one will earn both this world and the next. However, even the power to accept all that happens with love comes from God, for there is no existence besides Him!
א-להיך your God	then, you will be with Him, and will be His portion	By relating to God in this way you will be with Him by being similar to Him, i.e., living in His ways. Then, as a Jew, you will be called by His Name.

2. See note 12 below.

3. "At that time, there will be neither hunger nor war, neither jealousy nor competition. Goodness will be abundant and all delicacies will be as profuse as dust. The world will only be occupied with knowledge of God, and there will therefore be great wise men who will know hidden and profound things, and they will reach the highest human

levels of knowledge of their Creator, as it says, 'For the earth shall been filled with knowledge of GOD as water covers the sea' (Isaiah 11:9)" (*Mishneh Torah, Hilchot Melachim*, ch. 8:5).

4. The Book of Psalms concludes with the verse, "Every soul [נשמה] shall exalt God; praise God!" (Psalms 150:6). From the similarity between the word נשמה, "soul," and the word נשימה, "breath," the sages teach that a person must praise God for every single breath that he breathes (*Bereishit Rabah* 14:9).

5. As it says, "All my bones will say, 'GOD, Who is like You!'" (Psalms 35:10). This verse, together with the verse mentioned in the previous note, complement one another in our service of God. The phrase, "Every soul..." relates principally to the union of the first two letters of God's essential Name (*yud* and *hei*) by the positive actions that we do, while "All my bones..." relates to the last two letters of God's essential Name (*vav-hei*) by our repentance for doing evil (see our book in Hebrew, *Lev Lada'at*, p. 10, note 34).

6. The Ba'al Shem Tov explained that the verse, "Forever GOD, Your word stands in the heavens" (Psalms 119:89) refers to the fact that the words and letters of the phrase, "Let there be a firmament in the midst of the waters" (Genesis 1:6) stand firmly forever within the firmament of heaven and are forever clothed within all the heavens to give them life (*Tanya, Sha'ar Hayichud Veha'emunah*, ch. 1).

7. This is the state of the righteous at all times, as the Talmud states (*Berachot* 64a), "Torah scholars have no rest, neither in this world nor in the World to Come, as it says, 'They will go from strength to strength,' (Psalms 84:8)." The explanation of this according to Chassidut is that the righteous continue to rise from level to level in their attainment of Torah secrets even after their passing from this world. However, in the time of the resurrection of the dead, the souls of the righteous will return to their bodies to enjoy the ultimate eternal state of spiritual and physical contentment (*Tanya, Igeret Hakodesh* ch. 17). This can be compared to someone who designs and builds a beautiful mansion. During its construction, the person

enjoys a certain amount of satisfaction from the knowledge that, with its completion, he will be able to live in the comfort of his new home. This stage is the level of our living in this world, where we are constructing, as it were, a home for ourselves in the World to Come, after our passing. Arriving in the World to Come is a time for rejoicing in the novelty of our new home, as when the mansion is completed and the person makes a party to celebrate its completion, walking through the rooms and reveling in the features of each and every corner. The final and ultimate joy comes from actually moving into and living in his new home. This final stage is the stage of the resurrection when the person's soul is reunited with its physical body. The person will then be able to enjoy all the spiritual levels that his soul attained after death in a state of peace and comfort, no longer having to battle against the body's physical desires as is necessary in our present lifetime. Neither will the person be forever moving from level to level spiritually, for he will now be acquainted with all the levels and will be able to make use of his spiritual attainments at his leisure (Rabbi Dov Ber Schneerson, *Sha'arei Teshuvah, Sha'ar Hateshuvah*, 13a-b).

8. The exact timing of the appearance of the Mashiach is unknown and those who claim to have calculated the time of his appearance are not to be believed and "all of the [calculated] conclusions [to the exile] have already passed, and the matter [the ultimate redemption] is now dependant only upon repentance and good deeds" (*Sanhedrin* 97b; see also *Mishneh Torah, Hilchot Melachim*, 12:5). Even so, many of the signs mentioned in the Talmudic discussion there, indicate that the revelation of the Mashiach is very near, describing in particular that in the time just before the appearance of the Mashiach there will be a great lack of respect among people and a lack of conscience and shame.

9. The idea that we should "live with the Mashiach" was one of the Lubavitcher Rebbe's most important teachings. He taught that the Mashiach is already here, and all that is incumbent upon us is to begin to see the world from this perspective. This is to be achieved

by studying all that pertains to the Mashiach and the ultimate redemption (see *Be'itah Achishenah*, pp. 13-14).

10. The twenty-four chapters of the Talmudic tractate of *Shabbat* correspond to the twenty-four hours of the day of Shabbat, thus the seventh chapter ("all sevenths are beloved"), corresponds to the seventh hour from midnight to the first hour after midnight. This is a most opportune time when the gates of Gan Eden are opened.

The numerical value of the term for Shabbat night in Hebrew (ליל שבת קדש) equals 1,176. 1,176 is the triangle of 48 (sum of all integers from 1 to 48). It is also the numerical value of the opening phrase of Maimonides' work, *Mishneh Torah*: "The foundation of foundations and the pillar of wisdom" (יסוד היסודות ועמוד החכמות), the initial letters of which spell out God's essential Name, *Havayah*. As Maimonides continues to explain, "The foundation of foundations and the pillar of wisdoms" is to know that God is the ultimate source of all reality. This is the knowledge that comes to the soul on Shabbat night.

The initial letters of the expression ליל שבת קדש permute to form the word "shekel" (שקל), the standard coin of the Torah (relating to Efron's four hundred silver shekels; see note 15, below).

The numerical value of the word "Shabbat" (שבת) alone equals 702, which is equal to 27 times 26 (the value of God's essential Name). 702 is the "diamond" of 26 (double triangle; the sum of all integers from 1 to 26 plus all the integers from 26 back to 1), relating once again to the value of the Name, *Havayah*.

Another special phenomenon relating to the numerical value of "Shabbat" (שבת; 702) is that, when its digits are reversed, the number becomes the numerical value of the word "light" (אור; 207).

11. The more that one illuminates the *sefirah* of acknowledgment by accepting all that happens to him wholeheartedly, with true simplicity, the more the inner energy of the *sefirah* of understanding shines into his psyche, thereby causing him to experience joy. This is the secret of the connection between the *sefirah* of understanding, whose inner experience is joy, and the *sefirah* of acknowledgment, as

stated in Kabbalah "understanding extends to acknowledgment" (*Etz Chaim*, 29:8; see also our book in Hebrew, *Hanefesh*, pp. 188ff).

12. Exodus 34:6. The relevance of the number 13 here is explained in the framed text, above.

Of the thirteen synonyms for "light," five end with the letters *hei-reish* (הר), including "purity" (טהר). Purity of the heart is one of the qualities necessary to allow its inner qualities to shine out to the world.

Zohar (זהר) is exactly the type of light you experienced, brilliant white with colors.

13. Isaiah 52:8.

14. Rabbi Abraham Abulafia, in the introduction to his book *Or Hasechel*, uses two expressions to explain the abstract quality of the mind: "bodiless" (אינו גוף) and "not a power of the body" (ולא בכח הגוף). Amazingly, the numerical value of each of these expressions equals exactly 156, the value of ציון (Zion)! This indicates the fact that just as God is the light that illuminates Zion (i.e. Jerusalem; *Bereishit Rabah, Chayei Sarah*, 59:5.) so too, the Divinely rooted superconscious illuminates the mind.

The sum of the remaining words of the verse is 689 (13 times 53) which is also the numerical value of the phrase "Eternity of Israel" (נצח ישראל) an appellation of God that relates to the revelation of the *mashiach ben David*. We can thus further understand that with the coming of the Mashiach, the Divine Presence that is hidden within current reality will be eternally revealed to mankind.

15. Genesis 23:16. The numerical value of the name Efron (עפרן) also equals 400. The root of Efron in Hebrew means dust, representing the qualities of laziness and sadness, which you seek to rectify by your Torah study.

The phrase that summarizes the transaction between Abraham and Efron is, "Four hundred silver shekels, in negotiable currency." This phrase has a numerical value of 1,880, while the term referring to

God's ability to pardon (וחנון), equals 120. When these two numbers are added together, alluding to the rectification of Efron, they equal 2,000 which equals 400 times 5. The number 5 alludes to the sages' interpretation of the verse "This is the history of the heavens and the earth when they were created." The word meaning "when they were created" is written בהבראם, which, the sages teach, can also be read to mean that the world was created with the letter *hei*, which has a numerical value of 5. A second interpretation of the word בהבראם is achieved by permuting the letters to read באברהם, referring to Abraham who personifies the character trait of loving-kindness, without which the world could not exist.

2,000 is also the numerical value of the large letter *beit* that is the first letter of the Torah

16. *Sha'ar Ma'amarei Rashbi*, commentary on *Sifra Detzniuta*, 1.

17. Daniel 12:3.

18. Ezekiel 1:14.

19. See our book in Hebrew, *Nefesh Beriyah*, part 2, chs. 1, 2 and 6.

Glossary

Note: all foreign terms are Hebrew unless otherwise indicated. Terms preceded by an asterisk have their own entries.

Adam Kadmon: See **partzuf.*

Amidah (עֲמִידָה, "standing"): the central core and highest point of every prayer service. It is recited as a silent devotion while standing, feet together, facing Jerusalem. The weekday version consists of nineteen blessings; the Sabbath and holiday versions consist of seven, and the version of the *Musaf* of *Rosh HaShanah* consists of nine.

Arich Anpin: See **partzuf.*

Asiyah: See **worlds.*

Atik Yomin: See **partzuf.*

Atzilut: See **worlds.*

Ba'al Shem Tov (בַּעַל שֵׁם טוֹב, "Master of the Good Name [of God]"): Title of Rabbi Israel ben Eliezer (1698-1760), founder of the Chassidic movement (see *Chassidut*).

Ba'al teshuvah (בַּעַל תְּשׁוּבָה, "one who returns"): one who returns to the ways of Judaism and adherence to Jewish law after a period of estrangement. Often used in contrast to a **tzadik,* who has not undergone such a period. The *ba'al teshuvah* strives continually to ascend, return and become merged and included within God's essence; the *tzadik* strives primarily to serve God by doing good deeds and thus drawing His light into the world. Ideally these two paths are meant to be inter-included, i.e. every Jew should embody both the service of the *ba'al teshuvah* as well as that of the *tzadik*. See also *teshuvah.*

Beriah: See *worlds.

Binah (בִּינָה, "understanding"): the third of the ten *sefirot.

Bitul (בִּטוּל, "self-nullification"): any of a number of states of selflessness or self-annulment. The inner experience of the *sefirah of *chochmah.

Brit (בְּרִית, "covenant") or *brit milah* (בְּרִית מִילָה, "covenant of circumcision"): 1. the covenant or eternal bond God made with Abraham and the Jewish people, indicated by the *circumcision of the male reproductive organ on the eighth day after birth. 2. The ceremony at which this commandment is performed. 3. Euphemism for the male reproductive organ itself.

Candelabra (מְנוֹרָה; *menorah*): the seven-branched candelabra situated in the sanctuary of the Holy *Temple in Jerusalem.

Chabad (חב״ד): 1. An acronym for the constellation of the three *sefirot associated with the powers of the intellect: *chochmah, *binah and *da'at; 2. Name of a branch of *Chassidut that emphasizes the role of intellect and meditation in the service of God, founded by Rabbi Shneur Zalman of Liadi (the Alter Rebbe); also called *Lubavitch.

Chaos: see *Tohu*.

Chassidut (חֲסִידוּת, "piety" or "loving-kindness"): 1. An attribute or way of life that goes beyond the letter of the law. 2. The movement within Judaism founded by Rabbi Israel Ba'al Shem Tov (1648-1760), the purpose of which is to awaken the Jewish people to its own inner self through the inner dimension of the Torah and thus to prepare the way for the advent of *Mashiach*. 3. The oral and written teachings of this movement.

Chesed (חֶסֶד, "loving-kindness"; pl. חֲסָדִים *chasadim*): 1. the fourth of the ten *sefirot. 2. a manifestation of this attribute, specifically in *da'at.

Chochmah (חָכְמָה, "wisdom" or "insight"): the second of the ten *sefirot.

Circumcision (מִילָה, *Milah*): 1. the rite of circumcision, performed on a Jewish boy on the eighth day after his birth. 2. specifically, the first phase of this rite in which the foreskin is cut.

Da'at (דַּעַת, "knowledge"): 1. the unifying force within the ten *sefirot. 2. the third *sefirah of the intellect, counted as one of the ten sefirot when *keter is not enumerated.

Gematria (גִּימַטְרִיָּא, numerical value [Aramaic]): the technique of comparing Hebrew words and phrases based on their numerical values.

Halachah (הֲלָכָה, "way" or "walking"): 1. the entire corpus of Jewish law. 2. a specific Jewish law.

Havayah (הוי־ה): also known as the Tetragrammaton ("four-letter Name"). Due to its great sanctity, this Name may only be pronounced in the Holy Temple. When one recites a complete Scriptural verse or liturgy, it is read as if it were the Name *Adni*; otherwise, one says *Hashem* (הַשֵּׁם, "the Name") or *Havayah* (הֲוָיָה a permutation of the four letters of this Name).

Havayah is the most sacred of God's Names. Although no name can fully express the Essence of God, the Name *Havayah* does, in certain contexts, refer to God's essence. In these cases it is called "the higher Name *Havayah*" and is termed "the essential Name" (שֵׁם הָעֶצֶם), "the unique Name" (שֵׁם הַמְיֻחָד), and "the explicit Name" (שֵׁם הַמְפֹרָשׁ).

Otherwise, the Name *Havayah* refers to God as He manifests Himself through creation. In these cases it is called "the lower Name *Havayah*," and its four letters are seen to depict in their form the creative process and allude to the worlds, ten *sefirot*, etc., as follows:

		creation	*worlds	*sefirot
קוצו של יוד	upper "tip" of the *yud*	will to create	Adam Kadmon	keter
יוד	yud	contraction	Atzilut	chochmah
ה	hei	expansion	Beriah	binah
ו	vav	extension	Yetzirah	the six *midot*
ה	hei	expansion	Asiyah	malchut

The lower Name *Havayah* appears on several levels. It is first manifest as the light within all the *sefirot*. It thus possesses on this level ten iterations, which are indicated as ten vocalizations—each using one of the ten vowels. (These are only meditative "vocalizations," since it is forbidden to pronounce the Name *Havayah* with any vocalization, as we have said.) For example, when each of its four letters is vocalized with a *kamatz*, it signifies the light within the *sefirah* of *keter*; when they are each vocalized with a *patach*, it signifies the light within the *sefirah* of *chochmah*. The other Names of God (including the subsequent manifestations of the Name *Havayah*) refer to the vessels of the *sefirot*. In the World of *Atzilut*, where these Names are principally manifest, both the vessels and the lights of the *sefirot* are manifestations of Divinity.

The second manifestation of the lower Name *Havayah* is in the *sefirah* of *chochmah*. (This is alluded to in the verse, "*Havayah* in *chochmah* founded the earth" [*Proverbs* 3:19].)

Its third manifestation is as the vessel of the *sefirah* of *binah*. This manifestation is indicated by the consonants of the Name vocalized with the vowels of (and read as) the Name *Elokim* (for example, *Deuteronomy* 3:24, etc.).

The most basic manifestation of the lower Name *Havayah* is in the vessel of the *sefirah* of *tiferet*, whose inner experience is mercy. The Name *Havayah* in general is associated with "the principle of mercy," since mercy is the most basic emotion through which God relates to His creation. In this, its most common sense, it is vocalized with the vowels of (and read as) the Name *Adni*.

Hod (הוֹד, "acknowledgment," "splendor," "thanksgiving"): the eighth of the ten **sefirot*.

Ima (אִמָּא, "mother" [Aramaic] principle): the **partzuf* of **binah*.

Kabbalah (קַבָּלָה, "receiving" or "tradition"): the esoteric dimension of the Torah.

Keter (כֶּתֶר, "superconscious crown"): The first of the ten **sefirot*.

Lights: see *Sefirah*.

Lubavitch (ליוּבאוויטש, "City of Love" [Russian]): the town that served as the center of the *Chabad* movement from 1812 to 1915; the movement also became known after the name of this town.

Malchut (מַלְכוּת, "kingdom"): the last of the ten *sefirot.

Mashiach (מָשִׁיחַ, "anointed one," "messiah"): the prophesied descendant of King David who will reinstate the Torah-ordained monarchy (which he will head), rebuild the Holy *Temple, and gather the exiled Jewish people to their homeland. This series of events (collectively called "the Redemption") will usher in an era of eternal, universal peace and true knowledge of God, called "the messianic era." There is also a prophesied messianic figure called *Mashiach ben Yosef*, who will rectify certain spiritual aspects of reality in preparation for the advent of *Mashiach ben David*.

Mazal (מַזָל, "sign"; pl. מַזָלוֹת, *mazalot*): 1. a spiritual conduit of Divine beneficence (from the Hebrew root "to flow" [נזל]). 2. specifically, the thirteen tufts of the "beard" of *Arich Anpin. 3. a physical embodiment of such a spiritual conduit, such as a star, planet, constellation, etc. 4. specifically, the twelve constellations of the zodiac. 5. According to our sages, the Jewish People are not under the influence of the *mazalot*. The Ba'al Shem Tov teaches that the Divine "nothingness" itself is the true *mazal* of the Jewish People.

Midrash (מִדְרָשׁ, "seeking"; pl. מִדְרָשִׁים, *Midrashim*): the second major body of the oral Torah (after the *Talmud*), consisting of halachic or homiletic material couched as linguistic analyses of the Biblical text. An individual work of midrashic material is also called a *Midrash*, as is a specific analysis in midrashic style.

The *Midrash* is a corpus of many works written over the span of several centuries (roughly the second to the eighth CE), mostly in the Holy Land. The chief collection of homiletic midrashic material is the *Rabah* ("great") series, covering the five books of Moses and the five scrolls. Other important collections are *Midrash Tanchuma, Midrash Tehilim, Pesikta d'Rav Kahana, Pirkei d'Rabbi Eliezer* and *Tana d'vei Eliyahu*. Several later collections contain material that has reached us in its original form. These include *Midrash HaGadol* and *Yalkut Shimoni*. There are many smaller, minor *Midrashim*, as well; some of these are to be found in the collection *Otzar HaMidrashim*. Halachic *Midrashim* include the *Mechilta*, the *Sifra* and the *Sifrei*.

Mishnah: see **Talmud*.

Mitzvah (מִצְוָה, "commandment"; pl. מִצְוֹת, *mitzvot*): one of the six hundred thirteen commandments given by God to the Jewish people, or seven commandments given by God to the nations of the world, at Mt. Sinai. 2. one of the seven commandments instituted by the sages. 3. idiomatically, any good deed.

Mitzvot: plural of **mitzvah*.

Netzach (נֶצַח, "victory," "eternity"): the seventh of the ten **sefirot*.

Pardes (פַּרְדֵּס, "orchard"): an acronym for the four general levels of Torah study (פשט, רמז, דרוש, סוד; literal meaning, allusions, homiletic expansion and secrets).

Partzuf (פַּרְצוּף, "profile," "persona"; pl. פַּרְצוּפִים, *partzufim*): the third and final stage in the development of a **sefirah*, in which it metamorphoses from a tenfold articulation of sub-*sefirot* into a human-like figure possessing the full set of intellectual and emotional powers. As such, it may thus interact with the other *partzufim* (which could not occur before this transformation. This stage of development constitutes the transition from **Tohu* to *Tikun* (or from *Nekudim* to *Berudim*, see under Worlds).

The *sefirot* develop into a primary and a secondary array of *partzufim*, as follows:

sefirah	primary *partzufim*		secondary *partzufim*	
crown keter	עַתִּיק יוֹמִין Atik Yomin	"The Ancient of Days"	עַתִּיק יוֹמִין Atik Yomin	[The male dimension of] "the Ancient of Days"
			נוּקְבֵיה דְעַתִּיק יוֹמִין Nukvei Atik Yomin'd	[The female dimension of] "the Ancient of Days"
	אֲרִיךְ אַנְפִּין Arich Anpin	"The Long Face"	אֲרִיךְ אַנְפִּין Arich Anpin	[The male dimension of] "the Long Face"
			נוּקְבֵיה דְאֲרִיךְ אַנְפִּין Nukvei d'Arich Anpin	[The female dimension of] "the Long Face"
wisdom chochmah	אַבָּא Abba	"Father"	אַבָּא עִילָאָה Abba Ila'ah	"Supernal Father"
			אִמָּא עִילָאָה Ima Ila'ah	"Supernal Mother"
understanding binah	אִמָּא Ima	"Mother"	יִשְׂרָאֵל סַבָא Yisrael Saba	"Israel the Elder"
			תְּבוּנָה Tevunah	"Understanding"
the emotive sefirot midot	זְעֵיר אַנְפִּין Z'eir Anpin	"The Small Face"	יִשְׂרָאֵל Yisrael	"Israel"
			לֵאָה Leah	"Leah"
kingdom malchut	נוּקְבֵיה דְזְעֵיר אַנְפִּין Nukvei d'Z'eir Anpin	"The Female of the Small Face"	יַעֲקֹב Yaakov	"Jacob"
			רָחֵל Rachel	"Rachel"

Within any particular *partzuf,* the *sefirot* are arranged along three axes, right, left and middle, as follows:

left axis	center axis	right axis
	crown *keter*	
understanding *binah*		wisdom *chochmah*
	knowledge *da'at*	
might *gevurah*		loving-kindness *chesed*
	beauty *tiferet*	
acknowledgment *hod*		victory *netzach*
	foundation *yesod*	
	kingdom *malchut*	

In this arrangement, there are three triads of related *sefirot*: *chochmah-binah-da'at* (the intellect), *chesed-gevurah-tiferet* (the primary emotions) and *netzach-hod-yesod* (the behavioral attributes).

Perek Shirah (פֶּרֶק שִׁירָה, "Chapter of Song"): an ancient text, attributed to King David, composed of Biblical verses that articulate the songs of creation to God.

Rachamim (רַחֲמִים, "compassion"): the inner experience of the *sefirah* of *tiferet*.

Radla: see *Reisha d'Lo Ityada*.

Reisha d'Arich (רֵישָׁא דַּאֲרִיךְ, "the head of *Arich* [Anpin]" [Aramaic]): the lowest of the three heads of the *keter*, synonymous with the *partzuf* of *Arich Anpin*. In psychological terms, super-conscious will.

Reisha d'Ayin (רֵישָׁא דְאַיִן, "the head of nothingness" [Aramaic]): the middle of the three heads of the *keter*, related to the emotions of the *partzuf* of *Atik Yomin*. In psychological terms, super-conscious pleasure.

Reisha d'Lo Ityada (רֵישָׁא דְלֹא אִתְיָדַע, "the unknowable head" [Aramaic]): the highest of the three heads of the *keter*, related to the *keter* and intellect of the *partzuf* of *Atik Yomin*. In psychological terms, super-conscious faith in God.

Rebbe (רַבִּי, "teacher"): 1. a term used to describe or address a teacher of Torah. 2. leader of a branch of the Chassidic movement.

Ruach Hakodesh (רוּחַ הַקֹּדֶשׁ, "Divine inspiration"): a God-given ability of the righteous to correctly divine the implications of a given situation according to their own intuition; the first stage of prophecy as defined by Maimonides.

Sabbath: see Shabbat.

Sages: see *Torah*.

Sefirah (סְפִירָה, pl. סְפִירוֹת, *sefirot*): a channel of Divine energy or life force. It is via the *sefirot* that God interacts with creation; they may thus be considered His "attributes."

There are altogether eleven *sefirot* spoken of in Kabbalistic literature. Inasmuch as two of them (*keter* and *da'at*) are two dimensions of a single force, the tradition generally speaks of only ten *sefirot*. Each *sefirah* also possesses an inner dimension or experience, as discussed in *Chassidut*. The order of the *sefirot* is depicted in the chart on the following page.

Originally emanated as simple point-like forces, the *sefirot* at a certain stage develop into full spectrums of ten sub-*sefirot*. Subsequent to this, they metamorphose into *partzufim*.

Sefirot are composed of "lights" and "vessels." The light of any *sefirah* is the Divine flow within it; the vessel is the identity that flow takes in order to relate to or create some aspect of the world in a specific way. Inasmuch as all reality is created by means of the *sefirot*, they constitute the conceptual paradigm for understanding all reality.

Name			inner experience
כֶּתֶר	crown	אֱמוּנָה	1. faith
		תַּעֲנוּג	2. pleasure
		רָצוֹן	3. will
חָכְמָה	wisdom	בִּטוּל	selflessness
בִּינָה	understanding	שִׂמְחָה	joy
דַעַת	knowledge	יִחוּד	union
חֶסֶד	loving-kindness	אַהֲבָה	love
גְבוּרָה	might	יִרְאָה	fear
תִּפְאֶרֶת	beauty	רַחֲמִים	mercy
נֵצַח	victory	בִּטָחוֹן	confidence
הוֹד	acknowledgment	תְמִימוּת	wholeheartedness, sincerity
יְסוֹד	foundation	אֱמֶת	truth
מַלְכוּת	kingdom	שִׁפְלוּת	lowliness

Sefirot: plural of *sefirah.

Shabbat (שַׁבָּת, "Sabbath"): the day of rest beginning sunset on Friday and ending at nightfall on Saturday.

Shema (שְׁמַע, "hear"): a compilation of three Biblical passages (*Deuteronomy* 6:4-9, 11:13-21, *Numbers* 15:37-41) beginning with this word. The first verse is the fundamental profession of monotheism, "Hear O Israel, GOD is our God, GOD is one." We are commanded to recite the *Shema* twice daily, and it has been incorporated into the morning and evening services as well as the prayer said upon retiring at night. When reciting the first sentence, we are intended to consider ourselves ready to give up our lives rather than deny the oneness of God.

Soul: the animating life or consciousness within man (or any other creature, see *Sha'ar HaYichud VehaEmunah*, ch. 1). The Jew possesses an additional "Divine soul," an actual spark of Divinity, which is conscious of and focused on God's presence and will in creation.

The essence of the soul possesses five manifestations ("names"), as follows:

Name		Experience
יְחִידָה yechidah	"unique one"	unity with God
חַיָּה chayah	"living being"	awareness of God as continually creating the world
נְשָׁמָה neshamah	"breath"	vitality of intelligence
רוּחַ ruach	"spirit"	vitality of emotion
נֶפֶשׁ nefesh	"creature"	physical vitality

Talmud: (תַּלְמוּד, "learning"): the written version of the greater part of the Oral *Torah, comprising mostly legal but also much homiletic and even some explicitly mystical material.

The *Talmud* comprises the *Mishnah* (מִשְׁנָה, "recitation") and the *Gemara* (גְּמָרָא, "study"). The *Mishnah* is the basic compendium of the laws (each known as a *mishnah*) comprising the Oral Torah, redacted by Rabbi Yehudah the Prince in the second century CE. The *Mishnah* was elaborated upon over the next few centuries in the academies of the Holy Land and Babylonia; this material is the *Gemara*.

There are thus two *Talmuds*: the one composed in the Holy Land, known as the *Talmud Yerushalmi* ("The Jerusalem *Talmud*"), completed in the third century, and the one composed in Babylonia, known as the *Talmud Bavli* ("The Babylonian *Talmud*), completed in the sixth century.

The *Mishnah*—and *ipso facto* the *Talmud*—is divided into tractates. References to the *Mishnah* are simply the name of the tractate followed by the number of the chapter and individual *mishnah*.

The Jerusalem Talmud was first printed in Venice, 1523-24. Although subsequent editions have generally followed the same pagination as this edition, it is nonetheless cited by chapter and *halachah* (i.e., individual *mishnah*) number, as is the *Mishnah*. The Babylonian Talmud was first printed in its entirety in Venice,

1520-23, and subsequent editions have followed the same pagination as this edition. References to the tractates of the *Talmud Bavli* are simply by tractate name followed by leaf and page ("a" or "b").

Temimut (תְּמִימוּת, "wholeheartedness;" "sincerity"): 1. earnestness and sincerity, either in one's conduct with his fellow man or in his connection to God. 2. The inner experience of **hod*.

Temple (or "Holy Temple"; Hebrew: בֵּית הַמִּקְדָּשׁ, "house of the sanctuary"): The central sanctuary in Jerusalem which serves as the physical abode of the indwelling of God's Presence on earth and as the venue for the sacrificial service. The Temple is the focal point of one's spiritual consciousness. The first Temple was built by King Solomon (833 BCE) and destroyed by the Babylonians (423 BCE); the second Temple was built by Zerubabel (synonymous, according to some opinions, with Nehemiah, 352 BCE), remodeled by Herod and destroyed by the Romans (68 CE); the third, eternal Temple will be built by *Mashiach*.

Teshuvah (תְּשׁוּבָה, "return"): the return of the individual (or community), after a period of estrangement, to a state of oneness with and commitment to God and His Torah. See **Ba'al Teshuvah*.

Tiferet (תִּפְאֶרֶת, "beauty"): the sixth of the ten **sefirot*.

Tohu (תֹּהוּ, "chaos"): 1. the primordial, unrectified state of creation. 2. "The world of *Tohu*" is the **world* which manifests this state, synonymous with the initial, premature form of the world of **Atzilut*. It itself develops in two stages: a stable form (*Akudim*) followed by an unstable form (*Nekudim*, see Worlds). The world of *Tohu* is characterized by "great lights" entering premature "vessels," resulting in the (שְׁבִירַת הַכֵּלִים) "breaking of the vessels." See *Tikun*.

Torah (תּוֹרָה, "teaching"): God's will and wisdom as communicated to man. It pre-existed creation, and God used the Torah as His blueprint in creating the world.

God gave the Torah to mankind c. 1313 BCE (and during the ensuing 40 years) at Mt. Sinai through Moses. The Ten

Commandments were pronounced in the presence of the entire Jewish people.

God gave the Torah in two parts: the Written Torah and the Oral Torah. The Written Torah originally consisted of the Five Books of Moses (the "Pentateuch"), the other books being added later (see Bible). The Oral Torah was communicated together with the Five Books of Moses as an explanation of the laws and lore included in it. This material was later written down by the sages of the Oral Torah in the form of the *Talmud, the *Midrash, and the *Zohar. (All references to "the sages" in this book refer to the sages who transmitted the Oral Torah as recorded in these works.)

Triangle (of n): the sum of the integers from 1 to a specific number, n. For example, the triangle of 5 (denoted $\Delta 5$) is $15 = 1 + 2 + 3 + 4 + 5$.

Tzadik (צַדִיק, "righteous" person; pl. צַדִיקִים, *tzadikim*): someone who has fully overcome the evil inclination of his animal soul and has converted its potential into good.

Tzadikim: plural of *tzadik.

World (Hebrew: עוֹלָם): a spiritual level of creation, representing a rung on the continuum of consciousness or awareness of God. In general, there are four worlds: *Atzilut, *Beriah, *Yetzirah, and *Asiyah. In particular, however, these four worlds originate from a fifth, higher world, *Adam Kadmon. All ten *sefirot and twelve *partzufim are manifest in each world; however, since there is a one-to-one correspondence between the worlds and the sefirot, a particular sefirah dominates in each world.

The world of Atzilut is fundamentally different from the three subsequent worlds in that in it there is no awareness of self per se, while the three lower worlds are progressive stages in the development of self-awareness.

The worlds correspond to the Name *Havayah and the *sefirot as follows:

the Name *Havayah*	World	dominant *sefirah*	level of consciousness
קוצו של י	אָדָם קַדְמוֹן *Adam Kadmon* "Primordial Man"	crown	Divine will to create and plan of creation
י	אֲצִילוּת *Atzilut* "Emanation"	wisdom	solely of God; no self-awareness
ה	בְּרִיאָה *Beriah* "Creation"	understanding	potential existence; formless substance
ו	יְצִירָה *Yetzirah* "Formation"	the six emotive *sefirot*	general existence: archetypes, species
ה	עֲשִׂיָּה *Asiyah* "Action"	kingdom	particular existence; individual creatures

In particular, the world of *Atzilut* develops out of *Adam Kadmon* in three stages (the names of which are taken from *Genesis* 30:10):

world		developmental stage	description	
עֲקֻדִּים *Akudim*	"bound," "striped"	ten lights in one vessel	stable chaos	תֹּהוּ *Tohu*
נְקֻדִּים *Nekudim*	"dotted," "spotted"	ten lights in ten vessels, unstable	unstable chaos, collapse	
בְּרֻדִּים *Berudim*	"patterned," "speckled"	ten lights in ten inter-included vessels; stable	stable, mature rectification	תִּקּוּן *Tikun*

Whenever unqualified reference is made to the world of *Atzilut*, its final, mature stage is meant. It should be noted as well that our physical universe is below and "enclothes" the final two *sefirot* (**yesod* and **malchut*) of the spiritual world of *Asiyah* referred to above.

Yesod (יְסוֹד, "foundation"): the ninth of the ten **sefirot*.

Yetzirah (יְצִירָה, "formation"): one of the four **worlds*.

Yom Kippur (יוֹם כִּפּוּר, "Day of Atonement"): the holiest day of the Jewish year, marked by fasting and **teshuvah*, particularly through confession of sin.

Zohar (זֹהַר, "Brilliance"): one of the basic texts of the oral **Torah* and Kabbalah, recording the mystical teachings of Rabbi Shimon bar Yochai (2nd century). The Zoharic literature includes the *Zohar* proper, the *Tikunei Zohar*, and the *Zohar Chadash*. The *Zohar* was printed in 1558 in both Mantua and Cremona, but standard pagination follows the Mantua edition.

Subject Index

Bibliographic Index

Proper Names Index

Gematria Index